Handbook of
Business
Quotations

Handbook of Business Quotations

Choice Words of Business Wisdom for Successful Speeches, Reports, Letters, and Papers

Compiled by
Charles Robert Lightfoot

Gulf Publishing Company
Houston, London, Paris, Zurich, Tokyo

Handbook of Business Quotations

Library of Congress Cataloging-in-Publication Data

Hankbook of business quotations/compiled by Charles
   Robert Lightfoot.
       p.   cm.
   Includes bibliographical references and index.
   ISBN 0-87201-065-1
   1. Business—Quotations, maxims, etc.
I. Lightfoot, Charles Robert.
PN6084.B87H36   1991   90-3569
808.88′2—dc20   CIP

Quotes are reproduced in their original form. Authors' references to ''man'' and ''men'' apply to the universal sense of the terms, and are meant to encompass all people.

For
Charles Frank Lightfoot

Contents

∾ A ∽

∾ B ∽

∾ **Q** ∾

∾ **R** ∾

∾ **S** ∾

∾ **T** ∾

∽ **Preface** ∽

"By necessity, by proclivity, and by delight, we all quote."

—*Ralph Waldo Emerson*

"When a thing has been said, and well said, have no scruple; take it and copy it."

—*Anatole France*

Authors frequently begin a chapter with a quote. Often that singular quotation has more substance than the entire text that follows it. That is why I collect business quotations.

Charles Robert Lightfoot

Charles Robert Lightfoot
Canton, Georgia

Every man is a quotation from all his ancestors.

Ralph Waldo Emerson

∽ **Ability** ∾

There is only one proof of ability—results!

Harry F. Banks

He who has ability finds his place.

Charles Cahier

What one cannot, another can.

Sir William Davenant

Ability will see the chance and snatch it.

Arthur I. Guiterman

The greatest ability in business is to get along with others and influence their actions.

John Hancock

Abilities are like tax deductions—we use them or we lose them.

Sam Jennings

The greatest ability is dependability.

Bob Jones, Sr.

Ability is the heart to conceive, the understanding to direct, or the hand to execute.

Junius

To develop ease and confidence in doing, you must develop abilities and then develop excellence in the use of these abilities.

Phoda Lachar

Man is capable of all things.
Montaigne

Everyone excels in something.
Publilius Syrus

Executive ability is deciding
quickly and getting someone
else to do the work.
John G. Pollard

∾ Accomplishment ⌒

The mightiest works have been
accomplished by men who have
somehow kept their ability to
dream great dreams.
Walter Russell Bowie

Knowledge may give weight,
but accomplishments give lus-
ter, and many more people see
than weigh.
*Philip Dormer Stanhope, Earl of
Chesterfield*

There is no happiness except in
the realization that we have accomplished something.
Henry Ford, Sr.

To accomplish great things, we
must dream as well as act.
Anatole France

Who begins too much
accomplishes little.
German Proverb

Nothing is so fatiguing as the
eternal hanging on of an un-
completed task.
William James

The way to get things done is
not to mind who gets the credit
of doing them.
Benjamin Jowett

We would accomplish many
more things if we did not think
of them as impossible.
Chrétian Malesherbes

In accomplishing anything definite a man renounces everything else.
George Santayana

Who reflects too much will accomplish little.
Johann Friedrich von Schiller

∾ **Achievement** ✐

All that a man achieves and all that he fails to achieve is the direct result of his own thoughts.

James Allen

Nothing splendid has ever been achieved except by those who dared believe that something inside them was superior to circumstance.

Bruce Barton

Think of yourself as on the threshold of unparalleled success. A whole clear, glorious life lies before you. Achieve! Achieve!

Andrew Carnegie

Faith that the thing can be done is essential to any great achievement.

Thomas N. Carruthers

If we are to achieve we must look for the opportunity in every difficulty instead of the difficulty in every opportunity.

Walter E. Cole

The three great essentials to achieve anything worthwhile are, first, hard work; second, stick-to-itiveness; third, common sense.

Thomas Alva Edison

Open hands open the way to achievement. Put them to work today.

Wilfred A. Peterson

To achieve great things we must live as though we were never going to die.

Luc de Clapiers, Marquis de Vauvenargues

∾ **Action** ✐

Chaotic action is preferable to orderly inaction.

Anonymous

Honors and rewards fall to those who show their good qualities in action.

Aristotle

Action springs from a readiness for responsibility.

Dietrich Bonhoeffer

A man who has to be convinced to act before he acts is not a man of action.

Georges Clemenceau

The superior man is modest in speech, but surpassing in his actions.

Confucius

This is a world of action and not for moping and droning in.

Charles Dickens

This action makes the hero.

Oswald Dykes

Action and actions only determine the worth.

Immanuel Fichte

It is not enough to will, one has to act.

Johann Wolfgang von Goethe

Action takes precedence over study.

Judah Hanasi

Never confuse motion with action.

Ernest Hemingway

Seize the day, put no trust in the morrow.

Horace

Action will remove the doubt that theory cannot solve.

Tehyi Hsieh

All the beautiful sentiments in the world weigh less than a single lovely action.

James Russell Lowell

The test of any man lies in action.

Pindar

Do it if you're going to do it.

Plautus

Action takes away the fear of the act, and makes bold resolution the favorite of fortune.

Francis Quarles

Action is the basis of success.

Marie Beynon Ray

Action is eloquence.

William Shakespeare

Heaven ne'er helps the men who will not act.

Sophocles

Action is the first task of life.
William G. Sumner

Action makes more fortunes than caution.
Luc de Clapiers, Marquis de Vauvenargues

A life which does not go into action is a failure.
Arnold J. Toynbee

It is they who have the will to act who oftenest win the prizes.
Xerxes

∾ Activity ∾

Expect poison from standing water.
William Blake

Lose no time; be always employed in something useful.
Benjamin Franklin

It is better to wear out than to rust out.
Richard Cumberland

The used key is always bright.
Benjamin Franklin

Activity is contagious.
Ralph Waldo Emerson

You don't stand still. You either move ahead, or move backward.
Elisabeth Clairborne Ortenberg

∾ Adaptability ∾

When you are at Rome live in the Roman style; when you are elsewhere live as they live elsewhere.
Saint Ambrose

Take the tone of the company that you are in.
Philip Dormer Stanhope, Earl of Chesterfield

Meeting men or devils, talk as they do.

William Scarborough

Suit self to circumstances.

William Scarborough

Dance to the tune that is played.

Spanish Proverb

One should be compliant with the times.

Theodosius II

Adapt or perish, now as ever, is Nature's inexorable imperative.

H.G. Wells

Advancement

Build momentum by accumulating small successes.

Anonymous

If you want to go up, get down to work.

Anonymous

All rising to great place is by a winding stair.

Francis Bacon

Everyone can raise himself, but only by his own actions.

Nahman Bratziav

Like rowing upstream, not to advance is to drop back.

Chinese Proverb

It is necessary to try to surpass one's self always; this occupation ought to last as long as life.

Queen Christina

The best way to get out of a lowly position is to be conspicuously effective in it.

D. John Hall

If you add a little to a little and do this often soon the little will become great.

Hesiod

Gain access to the people on top. Until they know you, they can't help you.

Tom Hopkins

The rung of a ladder was never meant to rest upon, but only to hold a man's foot long enough to enable him to put the other somewhat higher.

Thomas Huxley

Let people see clearly that it is in their interest to promote yours.

Jean de La Bruyère

No one is going to win fame, recognition, or advancement just because he thinks he deserves it. Someone else has to think so, too.

John Luther

I found that the men and women who got to the top were those who did the jobs they had in hand, with everything they had of energy and enthusiasm and hard work.

Harry Truman

∾ Adversity ∾

Adversity introduces a man to himself.

Anonymous

The school of adversity is a very good school, provided you don't matriculate too early and continue too long.

Louis K. Anspacher

Adversity is sure to bring a season of sober reflection. Men see clearer at such times. Storms purify the atmosphere.

Henry Ward Beecher

Adversity is the first path to truth.

George Noel Gordon, Lord Byron

The diamond cannot be polished without friction, nor the man perfected without trials.

Chinese Proverb

The purest ore is produced from the hottest furnace, and the brightest thunderbolt is elicited from the darkest storms.

George Caleb Colton

There is no education like adversity.

Benjamin Disraeli

Grow hard, and stiffen with adversity.

John Dryden

When it is dark enough, men see the stars.

Ralph Waldo Emerson

Storms make oaks take deeper root.

George Herbert

Adversity has the effect of eliciting talents which, in prosperous circumstances, would have lain dormant.

Horace

Adversity reveals genius, prosperity conceals it.

Horace

Adversity is the source of strength.

Japanese Proverb

Advise and counsel him; if he does not listen, let adversity teach him.

Japanese Proverb

Prosperity is too apt to prevent us from examining our conduct; but adversity leads us to think properly of our state, and so is most beneficial to us.

Samuel Johnson

Into each life some rain must fall.

Henry Wadsworth Longfellow

The lowest ebb is the turn of the tide.

Henry Wadsworth Longfellow

Bloody noses are great teachers.

Joseph McKinney

That which does not kill me makes me stronger.

Friedrich Wilhelm Nietzsche

Fire is the test of gold; adversity of strong men.

Seneca

The gods are well pleased when they see great men contending with adversity.

Seneca

Sweet are the uses of adversity.

William Shakespeare

∼ Advertising ∽

Advertising is the mouthpiece of business.

James R. Adams

If you can keep your head while all others about you are losing theirs, you'll be the tallest one in the crowd.

Anonymous

If advertising encourages people to live beyond their means, so does matrimony.

Bruce Barton

In good times, people want to advertise; in bad times, they have to.

Bruce Barton

The advertisements in a newspaper are more full of knowledge in respect to what is going on in a state or community than the editorial columns are.

Henry Ward Beecher

In advertising there is a saying that if you can keep your head while all those around you are losing theirs—then you just don't understand the problem.

Hugh M. Bevill, Jr.

Doing business without advertising is like winking at a girl in the dark. You know what you are doing, but nobody else does.

Stuart Henderson Britt

The business that considers itself immune to the necessity for advertising sooner or later finds itself immune to business.

Derby Brown

The *Ancient Mariner* would not have taken so well if he had been called the *Old Sailor*.

Samuel Butler

The world runs on perceptions.

Alden W. Clausen

Advertising is what you do when you can't go see somebody.

Fairfax W. Cone

Advertising is the principle of mass production applied to selling.

John T. Dorrance

You can tell the ideals of a nation by its advertisements.

Norman Douglas

Advertising is based on the old observation that every man is really two men. The man he is and the man he wants to be.

William Feather

A good ad should be like a good sermon.

Bernice Fitz-Gibbon

The advertising man is a liaison between the products of business and the mind of the nation. He must know both before he can serve either.

Glenn Frank

An advertising campaign is only as good as the product behind it.

Howard Gold

Give them quality. That's the best kind of advertising.

Milton S. Hershey

An organized effort to extend and intensify craving.

Aldous Huxley

Promise—large promise—is the soul of advertising.

Samuel Johnson

The sign brings customers.

Jean de La Fontaine

It is the frequency of a message, not its length, that counts.

Leonard Lavin

A man's success in business today turns upon his power of getting people to believe he has something that they want.

Gerald Stanley Lee

Business today consists in persuading crowds.

Gerald Stanley Lee

Kodak sells film but they don't advertise film. They advertise memories.

Theodore Levitt

Advertising is the greatest art form of the twentieth century.

Marshall McLuhan

Advertising in the final analysis should be news. If it is not news it is worthless.

Adolph S. Ochs

The hidden persuaders.

Vance Packard

Advertising is not spending; it's an investment to get a piece of the mind of millions of Americans.

Alph B. Peterson

The true role of advertising is exactly that of the first salesman hired by the first manufacturer to get business away from his competitors.

Rosser Reeves

I can't think of a faster way to ruin a product than with advertising that's not truthful.

Joan Seidman

When someone stops advertising, someone stops buying. When someone stops buying, someone stops selling. When someone stops selling, someone stops making. When someone stops making, someone stops earning. When someone stops earning, someone stops buying. (Think it over.)

Edwin H. Stuart

Get the word out, you can have the most wonderful product in the world, but if people don't know about it, it's not going to be worth much.

Donald Trump

Many a small thing has been made large by the right kind of advertising.

Mark Twain

Half the money I spend on advertising is wasted, and the trouble is I don't know which half.

John Wanamaker

∾ Advice ᔆ

Never trust the advice of a man in difficulties.

Aesop

Beware of unsolicited advice.

Akiba ben Joseph

Had I been present at the creation, I would have given some useful hints for the better ordering of the universe.

Alfonso X

Be wary of people who want to rush in with advice.

Ann Beattie

Advice is a drug on the market; the supply always exceeds the demand.

Josh Billings

Who cannot give good counsel? 'tis cheap, it costs them nothing.

Robert Burton

Advice is seldom welcome; and those who want it most always like it least.

Philip Dormer Stanhope, Earl of Chesterfield

Nobody can give you wiser advice than yourself.

Cicero

To profit from good advice requires more wisdom than to give it.

John Churton Collins

He who builds to every man's advice will have a crooked house.

Danish Proverb

There are exceptions to all rules, but it seldom answers to follow the advice of an opponent.

Benjamin Disraeli

Don't give your advice before you are called upon.

Desiderius Erasmus

The wisest men follow their own direction.

Euripides

Those who counsel do not pay.

Flemish Proverb

He that won't be counselled can't be helped.

Benjamin Franklin

To accept good advice is but to increase one's own ability.

Johann Wolfgang von Goethe

None is so perfect that he does not need at times the advice of others.

Baltasar Gracián

Whatever advice you give, be brief.

Horace

A good scare is worth more to a man than good advice.

Edgar Watson Howe

He that is taught only by himself has a fool for master.

Ben Johnson

After I get the best advice available to me, I try to follow it.

Lyndon B. Johnson

A wise man puts aside 10 percent of the money he gets—and 90 percent of the free advice.

Harry Karns

It is easier to be wise for others than for ourselves.

François, Duc de La Rochefoucauld

Nothing is given so profusely as advice.

François, Duc de La Rochefoucauld

You will always find some Eskimos ready to instruct the Congolese on how to cope with heat waves.

Stanislaw Lec

Hazard not your wealth on a poor man's advice.

Francisco Manuel

Throughout my career, the things I've done best are the things people told me couldn't be done.

H. Ross Perot

A man who is always ready to believe what is told him will never do well.

Gaius Petronius

No man is wise enough by himself.

Plautus

Though men give their advice gratis, you will often be cheated if you take it.

George Dennison Prentice

Those who won't ask for advice most need it.

Publilius Syrus

Beware of advice—even this.

Carl Sandburg

It can be no dishonor to learn from others when they speak good sense.

Sophocles

No enemy is worse than bad advice.

Sophocles

A knife of the keenest steel requires the whetstone and the wisest man needs advice.

Zoroaster

∾ **Aggressiveness** ∾

The individual activity of one man with backbone will do more than a thousand men with a mere wishbone.

William J.H. Boetcker

We make way for the man who boldly pushes past us.

Christian Bovee

Be sure you're right, then go ahead.

Davy Crockett

Not only strike while the iron is hot, but make it hot by striking.

Oliver Cromwell

You can't achieve anything without getting in someone's way.

Abba Eban

Whatsoever thy hand findeth to do, do it with thy might.

Ecclesiastes

There is always room for a man of force, and he makes room for many.

Ralph Waldo Emerson

We all know that the nation can't divide more than the people produce, but as individuals we try to get more than our share and that's how we get ahead.

William Feather

Charging beats retreating.

Malcolm Forbes

You must either conquer and rule or serve and lose, suffer or triumph, be the anvil or the hammer.

Johann Wolfgang von Goethe

There is no shortcut to fame and comfort, and all there is is to bore into it as hard as you can.

Oliver Wendell Holmes, Jr.

Our strength often increases in proportion to the obstacles which are imposed upon it.

René Rapin

Don't foul, don't flinch—hit the line hard.

Theodore Roosevelt

Man is a fighting animal.

George Santayana

You don't learn to hold your own in the world by standing on guard, but by attacking, and getting well-hammered yourself.

George Bernard Shaw

To do anything in this world worth doing, we must not stand back shivering and thinking of the cold and danger, but jump in, and scramble through as well as we can.

Sydney Smith

Life is thickly sown with thorns, and I know no other remedy than to pass quickly through them.

Voltaire

∽ **Ambition** ઝ

The ambitious man climbs up high and perilous stairs, and never cares how to come down; the desire of rising hath swallowed up his fear of a fall.

Thomas Adams

There's always room at the top.

Anonymous

A man's worth is no greater than the worth of his ambitions.

Marcus Aurelius

Ambition is the growth of every clime.

William Blake

Ambition can creep as well as soar.

Edmund Burke

I had ambition not only to go farther than any man had ever been before, but as far as it was possible for a man to go.

Captain James Cook

From a little spark may burst a mighty flame.

Dante Alighieri

Life is too short to be small.

Benjamin Disraeli

Hitch your wagon to a star.

Ralph Waldo Emerson

Ambition is the mainspring of nearly all progress.

B. C. Forbes

'Tis laudable ambition, that aims at being better than his neighbors.

Benjamin Franklin

Who hasn't in his head a little grain of ambition?

Jean de La Fontaine

The amount of ambition a man possesses determines his place in the auditorium of life; whether he will be in the audience or on the stage.

Douglas Meador

Such joy ambition finds.

John Milton

He who does not hope to win has already lost.

José Joaquin Olmedo

Ambition hath no mean. It is either upon all fours or upon tiptoes.

George Savile

Hardly anything will bring a man's mind into full activity if ambition be wanting.

Sir Henry Taylor

Keep away from people who try to belittle your ambitions. Small people always do that, but the really great make you feel that you, too, can become great.

Mark Twain

Ambition's a good thing if you've got it headed in the right direction.

Josh Wise

Ambition is achievement.

Israel Zangwill

∞ **Analysis** ∞

Analysis kills spontaneity. The grain once ground into flour springs and germinates no more.

Henri Frédéric Amiel

Most new projects—I can even say every one of them—can be analyzed to destruction.

Georges Doriot

If you wait around for the anal-
yses to be completed—to get
even eighty percent of the
facts—opportunity has passed
you by.

Frank Lorenzo

To be a good trader, you have
to be disciplined and pull out
when your analysis goes
against you.

T. Boone Pickens, Jr.

It requires a very unusual
mind to make an analysis of
the obvious.

Alfred North Whitehead

∽ **Argument** ∽

Many can argue; not many
converse.

Amos Bronson Alcott

Silence is one of the hardest
things to refute.

Josh Billings

Behind every argument is
someone's ignorance.

Louis D. Brandeis

A man convinced against his
will is of the same opinion still.

Samuel Butler

The only way to get the best of
an argument is to avoid it.

Dale Carnegie

If you would convince others,
seem open to conviction yourself.

*Philip Dormer Stanfield, Earl of
Chesterfield*

The best way I know of to win
an argument is to start by
being in the right.

Quintin Hogg, Lord Hailsham

Prepare your proof before you
argue.

Samuel Hanagid

If you can't answer a man's argument, all is not lost; you can
still call him vile names.

Elbert Hubbard

The aim of argument should
not be victory, but progress.

Joseph Joubert

The pain of dispute greatly outweighs its uses.

Joseph Joubert

The greater a man's understanding, the further does he remove himself from quarrels.

Hasidic Saying

An argument is a collision between two trains of thought in which both are derailed.

Charles L. Lapp

We hardly find any persons of good sense save those who agree with us.

François, Duc de La Rochefoucauld

Keep cool and you command everybody.

Louis Antoine de Saint-Just

Arguments only confirm people in their own opinions.

Booth Tarkington

A long dispute means that both parties are wrong.

Voltaire

Keep cool; anger is not an argument.

Daniel Webster

❧ Aspiration ❧

What you are must always displease you, if you would attain to that which you are not.

Saint Augustine

Make no little plans; they have no magic to stir men's blood. Make big plans, aim high in hope and work.

Daniel H. Burnham

Every man believes that he has a greater possibility.

Ralph Waldo Emerson

'Tis but a base, ignoble mind that mounts no higher than a bird can soar.

William Shakespeare

In the long run men hit only what they aim at. Therefore, though they should fail immediately, they had better aim at something high.

Henry David Thoreau

∾ Attitude ∾

You will become as small as your controlling desire; as great as your dominant aspiration.

James Allen

Growl all day and you'll feel dog tired at night.

Anonymous

Instead of crying over spilt milk, go milk another cow.

Erna Asp

You can overcome anything if you don't bellyache.

Bernard M. Baruch

Life is a grindstone; whether it grinds you down or polishes you up depends on what you're made of.

Jacob M. Braude

Give to the world the best you have, and the best will come back to you.

Madeleine Bridges

Don't believe the world owes you a living; the world owes you nothing—it was here first.

Robert Jones Burdette

When fate hands us a lemon, let's try to make a lemonade.

Dale Carnegie

Make yourself necessary to somebody.

Ralph Waldo Emerson

Poverty consists in feeling poor.

Ralph Waldo Emerson

Work is done rapidly by willing hands.

James Anthony Froude

Be part of the answer, not part of the problem.

Buell G. Gallagher

Human beings can alter their lives by altering their attitudes of mind.

William James

The habit of looking on the bright side of every event is worth more than a thousand pounds a year.

Samuel Johnson

Where there is an open mind, there will always be a frontier.

Charles Kettering

There are really only three types of people: those who make things happen, those who watch things happen, and those who say, "What happened?"

Ann Landers

A willing mind makes a hard journey easy.

Philip Massinger

Always imitate the behavior of the winners when you lose.

George Meredith

Your living is determined not so much by what life brings to you as by the attitude you bring to life.

John Homer Miller

We are here to add what we can *to*, not to get what we can *from*, Life.

Sir William Osler

What we steadily, consciously, habitually think we are, that we tend to become.

John Cowper Powys

Whenever you are asked if you can do a job, tell 'em, "Certainly, I can!"—and get busy and find out how to do it.

Theodore Roosevelt

I feel that the greatest reward for doing is the opportunity to do more.

Jonas Salk

If we want a thing badly enough, we can make it happen.

Dorothy L. Sayers

I am as able and as fit as thou.

William Shakespeare

Let each man do his best.

William Shakespeare

The people who get on in this world are the people who get up and look for the circumstances they want and, if they can't find them, make them.

George Bernard Shaw

To be content with mediocrity is a tragedy.

Ruth Smeltzer

As long as a man imagines that he cannot do a certain thing it is impossible for him to do it.

Benedict Spinoza

There is little difference in people . . . the little difference is attitude. The big difference is whether it is positive or negative.

Clement Stone

There is nothing so easy but that it becomes difficult when you do it reluctantly.

Terence

I've never been poor, only broke. Being poor is a frame of mind. Being broke is only a temporary situation.

Mike Todd

What a man thinks of himself, that is which determines his fate.

Henry David Thoreau

We lost because we told ourselves we lost.

Leo Tolstoy

∾ Automation ∾

You must automate, emigrate, or evaporate.

James A. Baker

A tool is but the extension of a man's hand and a machine is but a complex tool, and he that invents a machine augments the power of man and the well-being of mankind.

Henry Ward Beecher

No machine can do the work of one extraordinary man.

Tehyi Hsieh

The more of the details of our daily life we can hand over to the effortless custody of automation, the more our higher powers of mind will be set free for their own proper work.

William James

Man is still the most extraordinary computer of all.

John F. Kennedy

You cannot endow even the best machine with initiative.

Walter Lippmann

It's going to be a tough decision when the purchasing agent starts negotiating to buy the machine that's to replace him.

Dave Murray

Truth and reason are common to all and no
more belong to him that spoke them heretofore
than unto him that shall speak them hereafter.

Montaigne

⤳ Beginning ⤳

A beginning is more than half
of the whole.

Isaac Arama

My way is to begin with the beginning.

George Noel Gordon, Lord Byron

The wise man, before beginning an action, looks carefully
to the end.

Bhartrihari

"Begin at the beginning," the
King said, gravely, "and go till
you come to the end; then
stop."

Lewis Carroll

Better never to begin than
never to make an end.

Thomas Braxee

Before beginning, prepare carefully.

Cicero

If the beginning is good, the
end must be perfect.

Burmese Proverb

Let us watch well our beginnings, and results will manage
themselves.

Alexander Clark

I start where the last man left off.

Thomas Alva Edison

Everyone who got where he is had to begin where he was.

Richard L. Evans

The way to get ahead is to start now. If you start now, you will know a lot next year that you don't know and that you would not have known next year if you had waited.

William Feather

Everything hath a beginning.

George Gasgoigne

No age or time of life, no position or circumstance, has a monopoly on success. Any age is the right age to *start* doing!

Lebrunie Gerard

Begin it, and the work will be completed.

Johann Wolfgang von Goethe

The century is advanced, but every individual begins afresh.

Johann Wolfgang von Goethe

Beginning is half way to winning.

Heinrich Heine

Once begun, a task is easy.

Horace

The journey of a thousand miles begins with one step.

Lao-tsze

Great is the art of beginning, but greater the art is of ending.

Henry Wadsworth Longfellow

It is not enough to begin, continuance is necessary . . . Success depends upon staying power.

James R. Miller

The births of all things are weak and tender, and therefore we should have our eyes intent on beginnings.

Montaigne

The beginning is the most important part of the work.

Plato

We all praise a good beginning.

Plato

Anybody can start something.

John A. Shedd

If one begins each task in a proper way, so is it likely will the ending be.

Sophocles

It's the job that's never started as takes longest to finish.

J.R.R. Tolkien

Look with favor upon a bold beginning.

Virgil

All glory comes from daring to begin.

Eugene F. Ware

The past is but the beginning of a beginning.

H.G. Wells

✺ **Boldness** ✺

Boldness in business is the first, second, and third thing.

Thomas Fuller

It is the bold man who everytime does best, at home or abroad.

Homer

In difficult situations the boldest plans are safest.

Livy

With audacity one can undertake anything.

Napoleon I

Audacity augments courage.

Publilius Syrus

No one reaches a high position without boldness.

Publilius Syrus

✺ **Budgeting** ✺

Budgeting: A method of worrying before you spend instead of afterward.

Anonymous

What you can do without a budget you can do better with one.

James L. Pierce

Earn a little, and spend a little less.

John Stevenson

~ **Business** ~

There is nothing more requisite in business than dispatch.

Joseph Addison

The man who minds his own business usually has a good one.

Anonymous

Business dispatched is business well done, but business hurried is business ill done.

Edgar George Bulwer-Lytton

The most important part of every business is to know what ought to be done.

Lucinus Columella

After all, the chief business of the American people is business.

Calvin Coolidge

Business civilizes the world . . . ties people together with the bond of mutual profit; discovers and rewards talent; awards prizes to genius . . . gives to the industrious and fair, dealing a sure reward.

John Cotton

Things that are bad for business are bad for the people who work for business.

Thomas E. Dewey

The man who is above his business may one day find his business above him.

Daniel Drew

Business? It's quite simple. It's other people's money.

Alexandre Dumas, the Younger

Business demands faith, compels earnestness, requires courage, is honestly selfish, is penalized for mistakes, and is the essence of life.

William Feather

All business is really the art of pleasing, and only the man or woman with the right kind of personality can please.

B.C. Forbes

Drive thy business, or it will drive thee.

Benjamin Franklin

The advance in business has been the greatest miracle the world has ever known.

Edgar Watson Howe

In the end, all business operations can be reduced to three words: people, product, and profits. People come first.

Lee Iacocca

The aim of all legitimate business is service, for profit, at a risk.

Benjamin C. Leeming

Business is a continual dealing with the future . . . a continual calculation, an instinctive exercise in foresight.

Henry R. Luce

Talk of nothing but business, and dispatch that business quickly.

Aldous Manutius

Be satisfied with your business, and learn to love what you were bred to.

Marcus Aurelius

Business in America should not be the captive handmaiden of government. It should be an institution responding efficiently to consumers in a free market.

James C. Miller III

One of the most important lessons of business—the value of concentrating on the customers you have.

Tom Monaghan

The secret of business is to know something that nobody else knows.

Aristotle Onassis

It either is or ought to be evident to everyone that business has to prosper before anybody can get any benefit from it.

Theodore Roosevelt

Keeping a little ahead of conditions is one of the secrets of business; the trailer seldom goes far.

Charles M. Schwab

Love what you're doing, because that's the only way you'll ever be really good at it.

Fred Trump

Business is like riding a bicycle. Either you keep moving or you fall down.

John David Wright

Who likes not his business, his business likes not him.

Thomas Wright

Go to your business, pleasure, whilst I go to my pleasure, business.

William Wycherley

I think we must quote whenever we feel that the allusion is interesting or helpful or amusing.

Clifton Fadiman

⤳ Capitalism ⤳

Capital is to the progress of society what gas is to a car.

James Truslow Adams

The strongest objection socialists and communists have against capital is that they don't have any.

Anonymous

Capital can do nothing without brains to direct it.

J. Ogden Armour

The capitalist system does not guarantee that everybody will become rich, but it guarantees that anybody *can* become rich.

Raul R. de Sales

Capitalism is based on self-interest and self-esteem; it holds integrity and trustworthiness as cardinal virtues and makes them pay off in the marketplace.

Alan Greenspan

And the word is Capitalism. We are too mealy-mouthed. We fear the word Capitalism is unpopular. So we talk about the "free enterprise system" and run to cover in the folds of the flag and talk about the American Way of Life.

Eric A. Johnston

Capital has its rights, which are as worthy of protection as any other rights.

Abraham Lincoln

The capitalistic system is the oldest system in the world, and any system that has weathered the gales and chances of thousands of years must have something in it that is sound and true.

Nicholas Longworth

Capital is past savings accumulated for future production.

Jackson Martindell

Democratic capitalism, combined with industrial democracy, is unquestionably the best way of life for mankind.

David J. McDonald

It takes more than Capital to swing business. You've got to have the A.I.D. degree to get by—Advertising, Initiative, and Dynamics.

Ken Mulford, Jr.

The system that has delivered more self-respect to more human beings than any other system devised by man deserves to be treated with more respect itself.

Richard M. Nixon

Capitalism is the power of stored money.

Carl Snyder

We cannot destroy the capital supply—whether by taxation or by other ill-advised policies designed to redistribute the wealth . . . without paying the piper.

Carl Snyder

∾ **Career** ᴄ

The man who selects the proper vocation in life has all the luxuries that life can provide.

Lloyd E. Bougham

Let him sing to the flute, who cannot sing to the harp.

Cicero

To find out what one is fitted to do and to secure an opportunity to do it is the key to happiness.

John Dewey

The best guarantee of a man's success in his profession is that he thinks it the finest in the world.

George Eliot

Each man has his vocation.

Ralph Waldo Emerson

First, say to yourself what you would be; and then do what you have to do.

Epictetus

Make your life a mission—not an intermission.

Arnold Glasow

Every calling is great when greatly pursued.

Oliver Wendell Holmes, Jr.

Who likes not his trade, his trade likes not him.

Frederick E. Hulme

Master a trade, and God will provide.

Midrash

Analyzing what you haven't got as well as what you have is a necessary ingredient of a career.

Grace Moore

Be a pianist, not a piano.

Alfred Richard Orage

All things are not equally suitable to all men.

Sextus Propertius

Take off your coat, and make dust in the world.

Charles Reade

Starting out to make money is the greatest mistake in life. Do what you feel you have a flair for doing, and if you are good enough at it the money will come.

Lord Rootes

A career, like a business, must be budgeted . . . a life that hasn't a definite plan is likely to become driftwood.

David Sarnoff

You cannot be anything if you want to be everything.

Soloman Schechter

Whatever you are by nature, keep to it; never desert your own line of talent. Be what nature intended you for, and you will succeed.

Sydney Smith

An aim in life is the only fortune worth finding.

Robert Louis Stevenson

Your identity and your success go hand in hand. Many people sacrifice their identities by not doing what they really want to do. And that's why they're not successful.

Lila Swell

Learn something, then you can go out and do it.

Ludwig Mies van der Rohe

As every divided kingdom falls, so every mind divided between many studies confounds and saps itself.

Leonardo da Vinci

Be whatever you want to be, but be it with all your heart.

David Wolffsohn

ᔕ **Caution** ᔓ

No one tests the depth of a river with both feet.

African Proverb

It is the part of caution not to be over-cautious.

Bahya ben Joseph

Caution, though often wasted, is a good risk to take.

Josh Billings

Look twice before you leap.

Charlotte Brontë

Let every man look before he leaps.

Miguel de Cervantes

Precaution is better than cure.

Sir Edward Coke

The cautious seldom err.

Confucius

Confident because of our caution.

Epictetus

He that will not sail till all dangers are over must never put to sea.

Thomas Fuller

Too much taking heed is loss.

George Herbert

He who wants the rose must respect the thorn.

Persian Proverb

He who hesitates is sometimes saved.

James Thurber

It is a good thing to learn caution by the misfortunes of others.

Publilius Syrus

Measure a thousand times and cut once.

Turkish Proverb

He that is over-cautious will accomplish little.

Johann Friedrich von Schiller

When in doubt what to do, he is a wise man who does nothing.

George John Whyte-Melville

∽ **Change** ∾

All great changes are irksome to the human mind, especially those which are attended with great dangers and uncertain effects.

John Adams

Action and reaction, ebb and flow, trial and error, change—this is the rhythm of living.

Bruce Barton

Change is the only thing any of us can count on.

Helen Gurley Brown

We change because we think we can do a better job. We also change simply to change. It's good to throw the cards up in the air once in a while. The results are often very healthy.

John Akers

We must all obey the great law of change. It is the most powerful law of nature.

Edmund Burke

Everything subject to time is liable to change.

Joseph Albo

The wise man does no wrong in changing his habits with the times.

Dionysius Cato

Don't ever take a fence down until you know the reason why it was put up.

> *Gilbert Keith Chesterton*

Change is constant.

> *Benjamin Disraeli*

There ain't no constants in business because people keep changing.

> *Solomon Dutka*

All is change; all yields its place and goes.

> *Euripides*

The sure path to oblivion is to stay exactly where you are.

> *Bernard Fauber*

We must always change, renew, rejuvenate ourselves; otherwise we harden.

> *Johann Wolfgang von Goethe*

The opinions of men who think are always growing and changing, like living children.

> *Philip G. Hamerton*

There is no way to make people like change. You can only make them feel less threatened by it.

> *Frederick Hayes*

Everything flows and nothing stays.

> *Heraclitus*

You cannot step twice into the same river, for other waters are continually flowing in.

> *Heraclitus*

The expert is usually the last to admit change, because he has so much invested in the status quo.

> *Charles Hess*

The world is changing at an incomprehensible speed, and that speed is accelerating all the time.

> *Tom Hopkins*

We must change to master change.

> *Lyndon B. Johnson*

The world hates change, yet it is the only thing that has brought progress.

> *Charles Kettering*

It is not inventions that put people out of work, but their own failure to change with the times.

> *Donald A. Laird*

The times change and we change with them.

> *Lothair I*

How many things served us yesterday for articles of faith, which today are fables to us.

Montaigne

Have no fear of change as such and, on the other hand, no liking for it merely for its own sake.

Robert Moses

The trick, of course, is to be alert to changes around you, to anticipate their impact on your institution, and then to respond; to reconceptionalize what you are up to.

John Naisbitt

We must drop the idea that change comes slowly.

Donald M. Nelson

O God, give us serenity to accept what cannot be changed, courage to change what should be changed, and wisdom to distinguish the one from the other.

Reinhold Niebuhr

All our final resolutions are made in a state of mind which is not going to last.

Marcel Proust

To avoid personal obsolescence, we must cultivate the ability to enjoy change rather than to resist it.

Lelan Russell

Progress is impossible without change; and those who cannot change their minds cannot change anything.

George Bernard Shaw

Consistency is the quality of a stagnant mind.

John Sloan

You have to have a program that's flexible enough to change rapidly, because rapid change is going to be the hallmark of the next 10, 20, 30, 40, 50 years.

Roger B. Smith

It will always do to change for the better.

James Thomson

It is better to be old-fashioned and right than to be up-to-date and wrong.

Tiorio

The most successful businessman is the man who holds onto the old just as long as it is good and grabs the new just as soon as it is better.

Robert P. Vanderpoel

The only man who can change his mind is a man that's got one.

Edwards Noyes Westcott

The past cannot be changed,
the future is still in your power.
Hugh White

Risky to change. Riskier not to.
John Young

There are no permanent
changes because change itself is
permanent. It behooves the in-
dustrialist to research and the
investor to be vigilant.
Ralph L. Woods

❧ Character ☙

A man is seldom better than
his word.
Lord Acton

A man has no more character
than he can command in a
time of crisis.
Ralph W. Sockmann

Listen to a man's words and
look at the pupil of his eye.
How can a man conceal his
character?
Mencius

Every cask smells of the wine it
contains.
Spanish Proverb

❧ Choice ☙

The strongest principle of
growth lies in human choice.
George Eliot

It is your conviction which compels you; that is, choice compels choice.
Epictetus

Regardless of circumstances,
each man lives in a world of his
own making.
Josepha Murray Emms

The world is full of cactus, but
we don't have to sit on it.
Will Foley

When you have to make a choice and don't make it, that is in itself a choice.

William James

Every man is the architect of his own fortune.

Sallust

∾ Commerce ∽

Commerce is the most important activity on the face of the earth. It is the foundation on which civilization is built. Religion, society, education—all have their roots in business, and would have to be reorganized in their material aspects should business fail.

James R. Adams

The only type of economic structure in which government is free and in which the human spirit is free is one in which commerce is free.

Thurman Arnold

Commerce: the greatest meliorator of the world.

Ralph Waldo Emerson

Commerce links all mankind in one common brotherhood of mutual dependence and interests.

James A. Garfield

Commerce: the equalizer of the wealth of nations.

William Gladstone

Perfect freedom is as necessary to the health and vigor of commerce, as it is to the health and vigor of citizenship.

Patrick Henry

Commerce is the great civilizer. We exchange ideas when we exchange fabrics.

Robert Ingersoll

Free commerce with all nations.

Thomas Jefferson

The propensity to truck, barter, and exchange . . . is common to all men, and to be found in no other race of animals.

Adam Smith

Nothing is more great or more brilliant than commerce: it attracts the attention of the public, and fills the imagination of the multitude; all energetic passions are directed towards it.

Alexis de Tocqueville

With the proper flow of commerce across the borders of all countries it is unnecessary for soldiers to march across those borders.

Thomas Watson

⟿ Common Sense ⟿

Common sense is the measure of the possible.

Henri Frédéric Amiel

Common sense is instinct, and enough of it is genius.

Josh Billings

Common sense is the best sense I know of.

Philip Dormer Stanhope, Earl of Chesterfield

Common sense is what the world calls wisdom.

Samuel Taylor Coleridge

Common sense is the shortest line between two points.

Ralph Waldo Emerson

Nothing astonishes men so much as common sense and plain dealing.

Ralph Waldo Emerson

Common sense is very uncommon.

Horace Greeley

It is a thousand times better to have common sense without education than to have education without common sense.

Robert G. Ingersoll

Common sense is not sense common to everyone, but sense in common things.

William James

One pound of learning requires ten pounds of common sense to apply it.

Persian Proverb

Fine sense and exalted sense
are not half so useful as common sense.

Alexander Pope

Common sense is the knack of
seeing things as they are, and
doing things as they ought to
be done.

Calvin E. Stowe

Success is more a function of
consistent common sense than
it is of genius.

An Wang

Common sense is Genius in
homespun.

Alfred North Whitehead

∾ **Communication** ∽

As soon as you are complicated, you are ineffectual.

Konrad Adenauer

Communication is depositing a
part of yourself in another person.

Anonymous

Nine-tenths of the serious con-
troversies which arise in life result from misunderstanding.

Louis D. Brandeis

To think justly, we must understand what others mean.

William Hazlitt

The most immutable barrier in
nature is between one man's
thoughts and another's.

William James

Good communication is stimu-
lating as black coffee, and just
as hard to sleep after.

Anne Morrow Lindbergh

Most of the grounds of the
world's troubles are matters of
grammar.

Montaigne

The articulate voice is more dis-
tracting than mere noise.

Seneca

Never whisper to the deaf or
wink at the blind.

Slovenian Proverb

You cannot speak of ocean to a well-frog, nor of ice to a summer insect.

Chung Tzu

Think like a wise man but communicate in the language of the people.

William Butler Yeats

❦ Competition ❦

Anybody can win unless there happens to be a second entry.

George Ade

May the better win.

Alcamaeon of Crotona

Competition is an economic struggle for survival among businessmen in which the consumer benefits the most.

Anonymous

Competition makes a horse race.

Anonymous

If you can't win, make the fellow ahead of you break the record.

Anonymous

The way to kill competition is to create something too good for competition to imitate.

Anonymous

Compete, don't envy.

Arabian Proverb

There isn't a plant or a business on earth that couldn't stand a few improvements— and be better for them. Someone is going to think of them. Why not beat the other fellow to it?

Roger Babson

No man prospers so suddenly as by others errors.

Francis Bacon

The folly of one man is the fortune of another.

Francis Bacon

Industry can be saved only by itself; competition is its life.

Honoré de Balzac

Even in a declaration of war one observes the rules of politeness.

Otto von Bismarck

He that wrestles with us strengthens our nerves and sharpens our skill. Our antagonist is our helper.

Edmund Burke

The first man gets the oyster, the second man gets the shell.

Andrew Carnegie

While the law of competition may be sometimes hard for the individual, it is best for the race, because it ensures the survival of the fittest in every department.

Andrew Carnegie

We will tackle the giants and set them back because we have a better product and better know-how of the marketplace.

Thomas Casey

The best mental effort in the game of business is concentrated on the major problem of securing the consumer's dollar before the other gets it.

Stuart Chase

Of all human powers operating on the affairs of mankind, none is greater than that of competition.

Henry Clay

Tradition approves all forms of competition.

Arthur Hugh Clough

I don't care so much about making my fortune as I do for getting ahead of the other fellows.

Thomas Alva Edison

The competitor to be feared is one who never bothers about you at all, but goes on making his own business better all the time.

Henry Ford, Sr.

We believe in competition, in the excitement of conflict and the testing of man against man in a fair fight.

Felix Frankfurter

He may well win the race that runs by himself.

Benjamin Franklin

I am firmly opposed to the Government entering into any business the major purpose of which is competition with our citizens.

Herbert Hoover

Don't knock your competitors. By boosting others you will boost yourself.

Jacob Kindleberger

Efficiency has this double edge—by its very success, it can crush competition.

Miles W. Kirkpatrick

Market competition is the only form of organization which can afford a large measure of freedom to the individual.

Frank Hyneman Knight

Man is a gaming animal. He must be always trying to get the better in something or other.

Charles Lamb

Promote yourself, but do not demote another.

I. Salanter Lipkin

I'm surprised how many people think you can throw a hand grenade at a competitor and expect he'll stand there and enjoy it.

Frank Lorenzo

Don't be afraid of opposition. Remember, a kite rises against, not with, the wind.

Hamilton Mabie

A horse never runs so fast as when he has other horses to catch up and outpace.

Ovid

Don't look back. Something may be gaining on you.

Leroy (Satchel) Paige

Compete, compete, compete— this is the keep-it-going spirit by which the person who tries will ultimately make records.

Norman Vincent Peale

The heart and soul of competing is knowing how to appeal to your customers. If you can't provide the products they really want, you won't succeed.

Donald Peterson

I don't meet competition, I crush it.

Charles Revson

Have five minutes more patience than your opponent, and you will be the victor.

Nicolas Risini

Human beings cannot be happy without competition, for competition has been, ever since the origin of man, the spur to most serious activities.

Bertrand Russell

I picture my competitor sitting at a desk in his opposition house, thinking and thinking with the most devilish intensity and clearness, and I ask myself what I can do to be prepared for his next brilliant move.

H. Gordon Selfridge

Do as adversaries do in law—
strive mightily, but eat and
drink as friends.

> *William Shakespeare*

Put yourself in competition
with yourself each day. Each
morning look back upon your
work of yesterday and then try
to beat it.

> *Charles M. Sheldon*

There is no resting place for an
enterprise in a competitive economy.

> *Alfred P. Sloan*

Men are not against you; they
are merely for themselves.

> *Jan Christian Smuts*

He who cannot swim must go
to the bottom.

> *Spanish Proverb*

Competition comes in place of
monopoly; and intelligence and
industry ask only for fair play
and an open field.

> *Daniel Webster*

There is perfect competition,
pure competition, imperfect
competition, monopolistic competition, non-price competition,
oligopolistic competition, cut-
throat or destructive competition, predatory and discrimina-
tory competition, unfair and
fair competition, and effective
or workable competition.

> *Clair Wilcox*

Some men are going to get
beaten because they have not
the brains, they have not the
initiative, they have not the
skills, and they have not the
knowledge, they have not the
same capacity that other men
have.

> *Woodrow Wilson*

∽ **Concentration** ∽

Concentration is my motto—
first honesty, then industry,
then concentration.

> *Andrew Carnegie*

The one prudence in life is concentration.

> *Ralph Waldo Emerson*

If you pursue two hares, both will escape you.

Greek Proverb

The highest preeminence in any one study commonly arises from the concentration of the attention and the faculties on that one study.

William Hazlitt

If you want to hit a bird on the wing you must have all your will in focus . . . you must be living in your eye on that bird. Every achievement is a bird on the wing.

Oliver Wendell Holmes, Jr.

When a man knows he is to be hanged in a fortnight, it concentrates his mind wonderfully.

Samuel Johnson

You have to train yourself to concentrate, and that's what I'm doing on the sidelines during a game. I don't see the game the way the fans do. I'm one play ahead all the time.

Tom Landry

The whole art of practical success consists in concentrating all efforts at all times upon one point.

Ferdinand Lassalle

Nobody can do two things at the same time and do them well.

Don Marquis

Even an angel can't do two things at the same time.

Midrash

Stick to one thing at a time.

Gaius Petronius

If you would be pope, you must think of nothing else.

Spanish Proverb

That man who concentrates all his energies of body, mind, and soul in one direction is a tremendous man.

Dewitt T. Talmage

My mind is a one-track road, and can only run one train of thought at a time.

Woodrow Wilson

∼ Confidence ∽

Confidence is keeping your chin up; overconfidence is sticking your neck out.

Anonymous

Confidence is the foundation for all business relations. The degree of confidence a man has in others, and the degree of confidence others have in him, determines a man's standing in the commercial and industrial world.

William J.H. Boetcker

Doubt whom you will, but never yourself.

Christian Bovee

Confidence is that feeling by which the mind embarks in great and honorable courses with a sure hope and trust in itself.

Cicero

Just as water rises no higher than itself, so the confidence of others in you will never be greater than the confidence you have in yourself.

Clinton Davidson

The first and great commandment is: Don't let them scare you.

Elmer Davis

The greatest builder of confidence is the ability to do something—almost anything—well.

Gordon Dean

The reward of one duty is the power to fulfill another.

George Eliot

The man who has confidence in himself gains the confidence of others.

Hasidic Saying

As is our confidence, so is our capacity.

William Hazlitt

Confidence or courage is conscious ability—the sense of power.

William Hazlitt

Skill and confidence are an unconquered army.

George Herbert

How do you build self-confidence? By making sure you win often enough.

Tom Hopkins

Confidence: The first requisite to great undertaking.

Samuel Johnson

Self-confidence is a virtue that should never lead to a single life; it should be wedded to tireless energy.

William G. Jordan

Bear in mind that self-confidence means a proper degree of self-management and courageousness . . . True self-confidence is always marked by simplicity and sincerity.

Grenville Kleiser

Confidence begets confidence.

Latin Proverb

Self-confidence carries conviction; it makes other people believe in us.

Orison Sweet Marden

You must do the thing you think you cannot do.

Eleanor Roosevelt

Lack of confidence is not the result of difficulty; the difficulty comes from lack of confidence.

Seneca

There's one blessing only, the source and cornerstone of beatitude—confidence in self.

Seneca

Show boldness and aspiring confidence.

William Shakespeare

Have confidence that if you have done a little thing well, you can do a *bigger* thing well, too.

David Storey

Men die of fright and live of confidence.

Henry David Thoreau

For they can conquer who believe they can.

Virgil

A man can be too confiding in others, but never too confident in himself.

Herbert H. Vreeland

∽ Consumer ∾

There's no consumer loyalty today; you have to make the shopping experience delightful.

Joseph E. Antonini

Consumers are the most merciless, meanest, toughest market disciplinarians I know.

Edwin S. Bingham

It is the customer, and the customer alone, who casts the vote that determines how big any company should be.

Crawford H. Greenewalt

The most important law in the whole of political economy is the law of "variety" in human wants; each separate want is soon satisfied, and yet there is no end to wants.

William S. Jevons

IBM always acts as if it were on the verge of losing every customer.

Jacques Maison-Rouge

Human wants are never satisfied.

J. Willard Marriott, Jr.

We have renewed our commitment to treating customers like human beings instead of numbers.

Michael McLoughlin

Scorn not the common man . . . thank God, he consumes.

Joseph Wood

It's the oldest lesson in the world: Unless you're customer-driven, you go out of business.

Walter Wriston

∽ Contract ∾

Remember, in every lease the big print giveth and the small print taketh away.

Anonymous

The fulfillment of the pledged word is of equal necessity to the conduct of all business.

James F. Bell

No man is bound by any obligation unless it has first been freely accepted.

Ugo Betti

My word is my Bond.

London Stock Exchange Motto

A promise made is a debt unpaid.

Robert William Service

∾ **Cooperation** ∾

One hand cannot applaud alone.

Arabian Proverb

Some men have a peculiar ability to know and to learn; some men excel others by their ability to have and to earn; some excel in producing things, others in creating ideas. They need each other.

William J.H. Boetcker

Proper cooperation cannot be secured between groups of men who are constantly quarreling among themselves over petty grievances.

Charles Gow

A dwarf on a giant's shoulders sees farther of the two.

George Herbert

Interaction among the different functions in a company is absolutely critical.

Lee Iacocca

Clapping with the right hand only will not produce a noise.

Malaysian Proverb

We are born for cooperation, as are the feet, the hands, the eyelids, and the upper and lower jaws.

Marcus Aurelius

Where there is unity there is always victory.

Publilius Syrus

We are apt to forget that we are only one of a team, that in unity there is strength and that we are strong only as long as each unit in our organization functions with precision.

Samuel Tilden

Cooperation is spelled with two letters—WE.

George M. Verity

Cooperation: Doing what the boss tells you, and doing it quickly.

Robert Zwickey

∾ **Creativity** ∾

Men must live and create.

Albert Camus

Creativeness often consists of merely turning up what is already there. Did you know that right and left shoes were thought up only a little more than a century ago?

Bernice Fitz-Gibbon

Creativity varies inversely with the number of cooks involved in the broth.

Bernice Fitz-Gibbon

Creative thinking may mean simply the realization that there's no particular virtue in doing things the way they always have been done.

Rudolf Flesch

The creative mind plays with the objects it loves.

Carl Gustav Jung

It is not the finding of a thing, but the making something out of it after it is found.

James Russell Lowell

It is man's nature to create as it is the nature of water to run down hill.

W. Somerset Maugham

We are what we create.

James Oppenheim

In order to compose, all you need to do is to remember a tune that no one else has thought of.

Robert Schumann

It is the critical spirit that creates.

Oscar Wilde

The individual is the origin of the great creative act.

Joseph C. Wilson

The baby creates the object, but the object was there waiting to be created.

Donald W. Winnicott

∾   **Credit**   ∾

Every dollar of fixed and stable value has, through the agency of confident credit, an astonishing capacity of multiplying itself in financial work.

Grover Cleveland

If you have cash today, you have credit tomorrow.

Confucius

In this institution of credit . . . always some neighbor stands ready to be bread and land and tools and stock to the young adventurer.

Ralph Waldo Emerson

Creditors are great observers of set days and times.

Benjamin Franklin

No man's credit is as good as his money.

Edgar Watson Howe

The creditor hath a better memory than the debtor.

James Howell

He who loses credit can lose nothing further.

Publilius Syrus

Credit lost is like a Venice-glass broken.

John Ray

Credit is like a looking glass, which, when once sullied by breath, may be wiped clear again, but if once cracked, can never be repaired.

Sir Walter Scott

The surest way to establish credit is to work yourself into the position of not needing any.

Maurice Switzer

Credit has done a thousand times more to enrich mankind than all the gold mines in the world. It has exalted labor, stimulated manufacture, and pushed commerce over every sea.

Daniel Webster

∾ Criticism ⌒

He who throws dirt always loses ground.

Anonymous

Sandwich every bit of criticism between two heavy layers of praise.

Mary Kay Ash

The legitimate aim of criticism is to direct attention to the excellent.

Christian Bovee

There's not the least thing can be said or done, but people will talk and find fault.

Miguel de Cervantes

I do not resent criticism, even when, for the sake of emphasis, it parts for the time with reality.

Sir Winston Churchill

Criticism, like rain, should be gentle enough to nourish a man's growth without destroying his roots.

Frank A. Clark

Criticism should not be querulous and wasting, but guiding, instructive, inspiring.

Ralph Waldo Emerson

Taking to pieces is the trade of those who cannot construct.

Ralph Waldo Emerson

If you have no critics you likely have no successes.

Malcolm Forbes

Criticism is most effective when it sounds like praise.

Arnold Glasow

The man who is anybody and who does anything is surely going to be criticized.

Elbert Hubbard

To avoid criticism, do nothing, say nothing, be nothing.

Elbert Hubbard

One should examine oneself for a very long time before thinking of condemning others.

Molière

Instead of criticism by speech, to show someone a better way to do a thing would be of much greater value.

John Wanamaker

Criticism comes easier than craftsmanship.

Zeuxis

⮀ Curiosity ⮀

"Curiouser and curiouser!" cried Alice.

Lewis Carroll

The important thing is not to stop questioning.

Albert Einstein

Curiosity is lying in wait for every secret.

Ralph Waldo Emerson

Curiosity is the root of knowledge.

Abraham J. Heschell

Inquiry is man's finest quality.

Soloman ben Judah Ibn Gabirol

Curiosity is, in great and generous minds, the first passion and the last.

Samuel Johnson

Curiosity is one of the permanent and certain characteristics of a vigorous intellect.

Samuel Johnson

The world is but a school of inquiry.

Montaigne

Look at all the sentences which seem true and question them.

David Riesman

No man really becomes a fool until he stops asking questions.

Charles P. Steinmetz

It is better to ask some of the questions than to know all the answers.

James Thurber

Judge a man by his questions rather than his answers.

Voltaire

The "silly question" is the first intimation of some totally new development.

Alfred North Whitehead

Speakers have been showering us with pearls of wisdom for centuries, and if all of their valuable advice were laid end to end, it would still be just as good as new.

Benjamin F. Fairless

∾ **Decision** ∽

The more alternatives, the more difficult the choice.

Léonor J. C. Soulas, Abbé D'Allainval

After all, it is better to be right 51% of the time and get something done, than it is to get nothing done because you fear to reach a decision.

Harvey W. Andrews

Failure to make a decision after due consideration of all the facts will quickly brand a man as unfit for a position of responsibility.

Harvey W. Andrews

A decision delayed until it is too late is not a decision; it's an evasion.

Anonymous

A decision is as good as the information that goes into it.

John F. Bookout, Jr.

Whenever you see a successful business, someone once made a courageous decision.

Peter F. Drucker

Decision is a sharp knife that cuts clean and straight; indecision, a dull one that hacks and tears and leaves ragged edges behind it.

Gordon Graham

A brief written presentation that winnows fact from opinion is the basis for decision making around here.

Edward G. Harness

If I had to sum up in one word what makes a good manager, I'd say decisiveness.

Lee Iacocca

There is no more miserable human being than one in whom nothing is habitual but indecision.

William James

Decision and determination are the engineer and fireman of our train to opportunity and success.

Burt Lawlor

The percentage of mistakes in quick decisions is no greater than in long-drawn-out vacillations, and the effect of decisiveness itself "makes things go" and creates confidence.

Anne O'Hare McCormick

The business executive is by profession a decision maker. Uncertainty is his opponent. Overcoming it is his mission.

John McDonald

The moment of decision is without doubt the most creative and critical event in the life of the executive.

John McDonald

Men must be decided on what they will not do, and then they are able to act with vigor in what they ought to do.

Mencius

Let go the things in which you are in doubt for the things in which there is no doubt.

Mohammed

Problems come when the individual tries to hand over the decision-making to a committee.

Rupert Murdoch

Nothing is more difficult, and therefore more precious, than to be able to decide.

Napoleon I

View decision-making as an art, not a science. It is better to be generally correct than precisely wrong.

Jill Neimark

There is no stigma attached to recognizing a bad decision in time to install a better one.

Laurence J. Peter

It is a very fine thing to have an open mind. But it is a fine thing only if you have the ability to make a decision after considering all sides of a question.

James E. Smith

Once a decision was made, I did not worry about it afterward.

Harry S. Truman

∾ **Deeds** ∽

All depends on deeds.

Akiba ben Joseph

Actions speak louder than words.

Anonymous

Business is like a wheelbarrow— it stands still until someone pushes it.

Anonymous

We live in deeds, not years.

Philip James Bailey

Do not seek to follow in the footsteps of the men of old; seek what they sought.

Matsuo Basho

Let us do or die.

Robert Burns

He that has done nothing has known nothing.

Thomas Carlyle

Men do less than they ought, unless they do all that they can.

Thomas Carlyle

As I grow older, I pay less attention to what men say. I just watch what they do.

Andrew Carnegie

The shortest way to do many things is to do only one thing at once.

William Cecil

Whatever is worth doing at all, is worth doing well.

Philip Dormer Stanhope, Earl of Chesterfield

Whatever you do, do with all your might.

Cicero

If I cannot do great things, I can do small things in a great way.

James F. Clarke

We cannot do everything at once, but we can do something at once.

Calvin Coolidge

Unless a man undertakes more than he possibly can do he will never do all that he can.

Henry Drummond

What is well done is done soon enough.

Guillame de Salluste, Seignor Du Bartas

Here lies Jack Williams; he done his damndest.

Epitaph in Boothill Cemetery, Tombstone, Arizona

What we do willingly is easy.

David Ferguson

Well done is better than well said.

Benjamin Franklin

Things don't turn up in this world until somebody turns them up.

James A. Garfield

Give me the ready hand rather than the ready tongue.

Giussepe Garibaldi

Knowing is not enough; we must apply. Willing is not enough; we must do.

Johann Wolfgang von Goethe

Whatever necessity lays upon thee, endure; whatever she commands, do.

Johann Wolfgang von Goethe

For every action there is an equal and opposite reaction. If you want to receive a great deal, you first have to give a great deal.

Ralph A. Hayward

You will probably get a larger position than you expect when you begin to do larger things than your firm expects you to do.

George D. Hobbs

A fellow doesn't last long on what he has done. He's got to keep on delivering as he goes along.

Carl Hubbell

There is no depression for good deeds, and that is all that business consists of, and that is our real business.

Henry N. Kost

Ask yourself always: How can this be done better?

Georg Christoph Lichtenberg

Something attempted, something done.

Henry Wadsworth Longfellow

We judge ourselves by what we feel capable of doing; others judge us by what we have done.

Henry Wadsworth Longfellow

Do not think that what is hard for thee to master is impossible for man; but if a thing is possible and proper to man, deem it attainable by thee.

Marcus Aurelius

No reward except for deeds.

Heresh Mathia

He who wants to do everything will never do anything.

André Maurois

It is not only what we do, but also what we do not do, for which we are accountable.

Molière

To know just what has to be done, then to do it, comprises the whole philosophy of practical life.

Sir William Osler

No need of words; trust deeds.

Ovid

Only deeds give strength to life.

Jean Paul Richter

Take the course opposite to custom and you will almost always do well.

Jean Jacques Rousseau

Say little and do much.

Shammai

Nothing is achieved before it be thoroughly attempted.

Sir Philip Sidney

Not theory but practice is the essential thing.

Simeon

It is the greatest of all mistakes to do nothing because you can only do a little. Do what you can.

Sidney Smith

And all that you are sorry for is what you haven't done.

Margaret Widdemer

∽ **Defeat** ∾

Defeat never comes to any man until he admits it.

Josephus Daniels

Man is not made for defeat.

Ernest Hemingway

The greatest test of courage on earth is to bear defeat without losing heart.

Robert G. Ingersoll

Believe you are defeated, believe it long enough, and it is likely to become a fact.

Norman Vincent Peale

What is defeat? Nothing but education; nothing but the first step to something better.

Wendell Phillips

A man is not defeated by his opponents but by himself.

Jan Christian Smuts

Defeat should never be a source of discouragement, but rather a fresh stimulus.

Robert South

Sometimes by losing a battle you find a new way to win the war.

Donald Trump

We are not interested in the possibilities of defeat.

Queen Victoria

∽ **Delegate** ∾

As soon as a man climbs up to a high position, he must train his subordinates and trust them. They must relieve him of all small matters. He must be set free to think, to travel, to plan, to see important customers, to make improvements, to do all the big jobs of leadership.

Herbert N. Casson

No matter how much work a man can do, no matter how engaging his personality may be, he will not advance far in business if he cannot work through others.

John Craig

If you don't take it for granted that the other man will do his job, you're not an executive.

William Feather

I learned along the way to delegate. I consider it the height of folly and vanity to try to do something that you can get someone else to do better—and that goes right on up to running the business if necessary.

Robert Fowler

I leave everything to the young men. You've got to give youthful men authority and responsibility if you're going to build up an organization. Otherwise you'll always be the boss yourself and you won't leave anything behind you.

Amadeo P. Giannini

No man is able of himself to do all things.

Homer

If you want work well done, select a busy man; the other kind has no time.

Elbert Hubbard

That man is great who can use the brains of others to carry on his work.

John R. Mott

∾ **Detail** ∾

If you do the little jobs well, the big ones will tend to take care of themselves.

Dale Carnegie

Beware of the man who won't be bothered with details.

William Feather

Paying attention to simple little things that most men neglect makes a few men rich.

Henry Ford, Sr.

Do well the little things now; so shall great things come to thee by and by asking to be done.

Persian Proverb

It is the close observation of little things which is the secret of success in business.

Samuel Smiles

We think in generalities, but we live in detail.

Alfred North Whitehead

∾ **Determination** ᔄ

A determined soul will do more with a rusty monkey wrench than a loafer will accomplish with all the tools in a machine shop.

Anonymous

Every good and excellent thing stands moment by moment on the razor's edge of danger and must be fought for.

Anonymous

Nothing great will ever be achieved without great men, and men are great only if they are determined to be so.

Charles de Gaulle

He only is a well-made man who has a good determination.

Ralph Waldo Emerson

Your degree of determination determines your outcome.

Malcolm Forbes

I have not yet begun to fight.

John Paul Jones

Where men truly wish to go, there their feet will manage to take them.

Talmud

∾ **Difficulty** ᔄ

Some men make difficulties, and difficulties make some men.

Anonymous

There are two ways of meeting difficulties: you alter the difficulties, or you alter yourself to meet them.

Phyllis Bottome

Difficulties are meant to rouse, not discourage. The human spirit is to grow strong by conflict.

William Elery Channing

The gem cannot be polished without friction, nor man perfected without trials.

Chinese Proverb

With stout hearts and strong arms we can surmount all our difficulties.

Henry Clay

A smooth sea never made a skillful mariner.

English Proverb

It is difficulties which show what men are.

Epictetus

Diligence overcomes difficulties, sloth makes them.

Benjamin Franklin

There are no gains without pains.

Benjamin Franklin

All things are difficult before they are easy.

Thomas Fuller

Nothing is easy to the unwilling.

Thomas Fuller

Difficulty is the excuse history never accepts.

Samuel Grafton

Every difficulty can be overcome.

Gabriel Hanotaux

Every difficulty yields to the enterprising.

Joseph G. Holman

Trouble creates a capacity to handle it.

Oliver Wendell Holmes, Jr.

Difficulty is, for the most part, the daughter of idleness.

Samuel Johnson

Make chariot wheels out of your difficulties and ride to success.

Bob Jones, Sr.

He who accounts all things easy will have many difficulties.

Lao-tsze

Exercise, exercise your powers; what is now difficult will finally become routine.

Georg Christoph Lichtenberg

I sometimes suspect that half our difficulties are imaginary and that if we kept quiet about them they would disappear.

Robert Lynd

I walk firmer and more secure up hill than down.

Montaigne

Undertake something that is difficult; it will do you good. Unless you try to do something beyond what you have already mastered, you will never grow.

Ronald E. Osborn

The best things are most difficult.

Plutarch

Have the courage to face a difficulty, lest it kick you harder than you bargain for.

King Stanislaus I

Nothing is so easy but it becomes difficult when done with reluctance.

Terence

What is difficulty? Only a word indicating the degree of strength requisite for accomplishing particular objects.

Samuel Warren

It is a good rule to face difficulties at the time they arise and not allow them to increase unacknowledged.

Edward W. Ziegler

When someone has the wit to coin a useful
phrase, it ought to be acclaimed and broadcast
or it will perish.

Jack Smith

∾ **Education** ∾

The essence of education is
overcoming a difficulty.

Alain

If you think education is expensive—try ignorance.

Derek Bok

Education is anything that we
do for the purpose of taking advantage of the experience of
someone else.

Lyman Bryson

Of the two purposes of education—to make a person fit for
the world as it is and to make
him able to change it—the second is the more important.

C. Delisle Burns

By nature all men are alike,
but by education widely different.

Chinese Proverb

Where there is education, there
is no distinction of class.

Confucius

Get over the idea that only children should spend their time in
study. Be a student so long as
you still have something to
learn, and this will mean all
your life.

Henry L. Doherty

It is the studying that you do
after your school days that really counts. Otherwise you
know only that which everyone
else knows.

Henry L. Doherty

If a man's education is finished
he is finished.

Edward Albert Filene

Your education begins when
what is called your education
ends.

Oliver Wendell Holmes, Jr.

I learned more about econom-
ics from one South Dakota dust
storm than I did in all my
years in college.

Hubert Humphrey

The object of education is to
prepare the youth to educate
themselves throughout their
lives.

Robert Hutchins

Education is no longer thought
of as a preparation for adult
life, but as a continuing process
of growth and development
from birth until death.

Stephen Mitchell

The best education in the
world is that got by struggling
to get a living.

Wendell Phillips

He is educated who knows
where to find out what he
doesn't know.

George Simmel

∽ Effort ∾

It is the amount and excellence
of what is over and above the
required that determines the
greatness of ultimate distinction.

Charles Kendall Adams

By labor fire is got out of a
stone.

Danish Proverb

Much effort, much prosperity.

Euripides

A business is never so healthy as when, like a chicken, it must do a certain amount of scratching for what it gets.

Henry Ford, Sr.

Any supervisor worth his salt would rather deal with people who attempt too much than with those who try too little.

Lee Iacocca

Few things are impossible to diligence and skill.

Samuel Johnson

Nothing comes from nothing.

Lucretius

No one knows what he can do till he tries.

Publilius Syrus

∽ Employee Relations ⌣

Much outcry, little outcome.

Aesop

You cannot raise a man up by calling him down.

William J.H. Boetcker

I praise loudly; I blame softly.

Catherine II

The real great man is the man who makes every man feel great.

Gilbert Keith Chesterton

To get the best out of a man go to what is best in him.

Daniel Considine

Our chief want in life is somebody who shall make us do what we can.

Ralph Waldo Emerson

People are more easily led than driven.

David H. Fink

I have found, in management, that people are the most challenging part of the equation. The people side has so many dimensions that it is more of an art than a science.

Hank Garmon

Correction does much, but encouragement does more. Encouragement after censure is as the sun after a shower.

Johann Wolfgang von Goethe

Treat people as if they were what they ought to be and you help them to become what they are capable of being.

Johann Wolfgang von Goethe

Few men ever drop dead from overwork, but many quietly curl up and die because of undersatisfaction.

Sydney Harris

It is easier to discover a deficiency in individuals . . . than to see their real import and value.

Georg Wilhelm Friedrich Hegel

Respect a man, he will do the more.

James Howell

Gain confidence of the people before laying burdens upon them; otherwise, they will consider it oppression.

Tzu Hsia

Don't mind anything that anyone tells you about anyone else. Judge everyone and everything for yourself.

Henry James

The art of being wise is the art of knowing what to overlook.

William James

Fail to honor people, they fail to honor you.

Lao-tzu

You can have all of the material in the world, but without morale it is largely ineffective.

George Marshall

Never discourage anyone who continually makes progress, no matter how slow.

Plato

You can accomplish by kindness what you cannot do by force.

Publilius Syrus

If you treat people right they will treat you right—ninety percent of the time.

Franklin D. Roosevelt

A word of kindness is better than a fat pie.

Russian Proverb

No man can ask more of a man than he is able to do.

John Scoggin

A smile in giving honest criticism can make the difference between resentment and reform.

Philip Steinmetz

You can employ men and hire hands to work for you, but you must win their hearts to have them work with you.

Tiorio

The sweetest of all sounds is praise.

Xenophon

∾ **Enthusiasm** ᔎ

The worst bankrupt in the world is the man who has lost his enthusiasm. Let a man lose everything else in the world but his enthusiasm and he will come through again to success.

Howard W. Arnold

When enthusiasm is inspired by reason; controlled by caution; sound in theory; practical in application; reflects confidence; spreads good cheer; raises morale; inspires associates; arouses loyalty; and laughs at adversity, it is beyond price.

Coleman Cox

Enthusiasm is the greatest asset in the world . . . it spurns inaction, storms the citadel of its object, and like an avalanche overwhelms and engulfs all obstacles.

Henry Chester

You can't sweep other people off their feet, if you can't be swept off your own.

Clarence Day

Merit begets confidence, confidence begets enthusiasm, enthusiasm conquers the world.

Walter Cottingham

Enthusiasm is that secret and harmonious spirit which hovers over the production of genius.

Benjamin Disraeli

If you want to be enthusiastic, act enthusiastic. Inner enthusiasm follows.

William Ellis

Every great and commanding moment in the annals of the world is the triumph of some enthusiasm.

Ralph Waldo Emerson

The simplest man, fired with enthusiasm, is more persuasive than the most eloquent man without it.

Franklin Field

Study the unusually successful people you know, and you will find them imbued with enthusiasm for their work which is contagious. Not only are they themselves excited about what they are doing, but they also get you excited.

Paul W. Ivey

If you aren't fired with enthusiasm, you will be fired with enthusiasm.

Vince Lombardi

Enthusiasm begets enthusiasm.

Henry Wadsworth Longfellow

The world belongs to the enthusiast.

William McFee

When a man has the gift of enthusiasm nothing can stop him.

Hal L. Nutt

If you can't get enthusiastic about your work, it's time to get alarmed. Enthusiasm must be nourished with new actions, new aspirations, new efforts, new vision.

Papyrus

Throw your heart over the fence and the rest will follow.

Norman Vincent Peale

None are so old as those who have outlived enthusiasm.

Henry David Thoreau

Apathy can only be overcome by enthusiasm, and enthusiasm can only be aroused by two things: first, an ideal which takes the imagination by storm, and second, a definite intelligible plan for carrying that ideal into practice.

Arnold J. Toynbee

∽ **Entrepreneurs** ∾

Treasure your entrepreneurs, because it is from their unfettered and sometimes undisciplined efforts that job creation will come.

David Birch

I am first and foremost a catalyst. I bring people and situations together.

Armand Hammer

Entrepreneurs search for—and create—value.

T. Boone Pickens, Jr.

American entrepreneurs are the men and women of faith, intellect, and daring who take great risks to invest in and invent our future.

Ronald Reagan

A man isn't a man until he has to meet a payroll.

Ivan Shaffer

Entrepreneurs are society's altruists. They're gift-givers.

David Silver

Entrepreneurs are gamblers, but the smart ones gamble on themselves.

James L. Sorenson

∽ **Excellence** ∾

Excellence is an art won by training and habituation. We are what we repeatedly do. Excellence, then, is not an act but a habit.

Aristotle

Excellence is not enough to know, but we must try to have and use it.

Aristotle

Each honest calling, each walk of life, has its own elite, its own aristocracy, based on excellence of performance.

James Bryant Conant

Excellence comes from men's rivalry with each other.

Ecclesiastes

All excellence involves discipline and tenacity of purpose.

John W. Gardner

Excellence in any art or profession is attained only by hard and persistent work.

Sir Theodore Martin

Only a mediocre person is always at his best.

W. Somerset Maugham

A man can do his best only by confidently seeking (and perpetually missing) an unattainable perfection.

Ralph Barton Perry

Thoroughness is a part of excellence.

Soloman Schechter

Better do a little well, than a great deal badly.

Socrates

All excellent things are as difficult as they are rare.

Benedict Spinoza

⚏ Excess ⚏

To go beyond is as wrong as to fall short.

Confucius

More than enough is too much.

Malcolm Forbes

The dinosaur's eloquent lesson is that if some bigness is good, an overabundance of bigness is not necessarily better.

Eric A. Johnston

Excesses accomplish nothing. Disorder immediately defeats itself.

Woodrow Wilson

⚏ Experience ⚏

Experience is more forceful than logic.

Isaac A. Abravanel

All experience is an arch, to build upon.

Henry Adams

Only when you have crossed
the river can you say the croco-
dile has a lump on his snout.

Ashanti Proverb

You may dispute principles, not
experiences.

Ludwig Boerne

You cannot create experience.
You must undergo it.

Albert Camus

The knowledge of the world is
only to be acquired in the
world, and not in a closet.

*Philip Dormer Stanhope, Earl of
Chesterfield*

It takes a lot of time to get experience, and once you have it
you ought to go on using it.

Benjamin M. Duggar

The years teach much which
the days never know.

Ralph Waldo Emerson

You take all the experience and
judgment of men over fifty out
of the world and there wouldn't
be enough left to run it.

Henry Ford, Sr.

Experience is not what happens
to a man. It is what a man
does with what happens to him.

Aldous Huxley

No man's knowledge here can
go beyond his experience.

John Locke

What happens to a man is less
significant than what happens
within him.

Thomas Mann

Only the one who eats the dish
knows how it tastes.

Midrash

The more sand has escaped
from the hourglass of our life,
the clearer we should see
through it.

Jean Paul Sartre

You shall know by experience.

Terence

We should be careful to get out
of an experience only the wisdom that is in it—and stop
there.

Mark Twain

Diamonds are not found in polished stones. They are made.

Henry B. Wilson

Other men are lenses through which we read our own minds.

Ralph Waldo Emerson

Facts

Facts, when combined with ideas, constitute the greatest force in the world.

Carl W. Ackerman

As a matter of fact is an expression that precedes many an expression that isn't.

Anonymous

Nothing can be more disputed than an indisputable fact.

Anonymous

Every man has a right to his opinion, but no man has a right to be wrong in his facts.

Bernard M. Baruch

If you get all the facts, your judgment can be right; if you don't get all the facts, it can't be right.

Bernard M. Baruch

Let us keep our mouths shut and our pens dry until we know the facts.

Anton J. Carlson

Facts are the most important thing in business. Study facts and do more than is expected of you.

Frederick Hudson Ecker

Get the facts, or the facts will get you. And when you get'em, get'em right, or they will get you wrong.

Thomas Fuller

The man who questions opinion is wise; the man who quarrels with facts is a fool.

Frank A. Garbutt

Facts do not cease to exist because they are ignored.

Aldous Huxley

I may act on my intuition—but only if my hunches are supported by the facts.

Lee Iacocca

Facts are stubborn things.

Alain René Lesage

Facts, if they are assembled upon a sufficiently partisan basis, can be made to document any case one wishes to establish.

James Henry McGraw, Jr.

All genuine progress results from finding new facts. . . . It is for us to discover them, and to learn the facts by which we can obey them.

Wheeler McMillen

Comment is free, but facts are sacred.

Charles Prestwick Scott

Get the facts first. You can distort them later.

Mark Twain

An ounce of fact means more than a ton of argument.

Marlin Vanbee

Every fact that is learned becomes a key to other facts.

Edward L. Youmans

∽ **Failure** ∾

Failure is not falling down; it is remaining there when you have fallen.

Anonymous

Failure is the line of least persistence.

Anonymous

It is an old saying that failure is the only highroad to success.

Graham Balfour

No matter how hard you work for success, if your thought is saturated with the fear of failure, it will kill your efforts, neutralize your endeavors, and make success impossible.

Charles Baudouin

Never permit failure to become a habit.

William Frederick Book

A failure establishes this: that our determination to succeed was not strong enough.

Christian Bovee

Self-distrust is the cause of most of our failures.

Christian Bovee

A man can fail many times, but he isn't a failure until he begins to blame somebody else.

John Burroughs

Men are failures, not because they are stupid, but because they are not sufficiently impassioned.

Struthers Burt

Ninety-nine percent of the failures come from people who have the habit of making excuses.

George W. Carver

He makes his failure certain by himself being the first person convinced of it.

Alexandre Dumas, the Younger

Show me a thoroughly satisfied man—and I will show you a failure.

Thomas Alva Edison

One principal reason why men are so often useless is that they divide and shift their attention among a multiplicity of objects and pursuits.

Nathaniel Emmons

Never be willing to adjust to failure, or you'll always be.

Malcolm Forbes

The opportunity to begin again, more intelligently.

Henry Ford, Sr.

We fail far more often by timidity than by overdaring.

David Grayson

Half the failures in life arise from pulling in one's horse as he is leaping.

Julius Charles Hare

Fail is made up of fear, apathy, indecision, and lack of purpose.

Tom Hopkins

The line between failure and success is so fine that we scarcely know when we pass it; so fine that we are often on the line and do not know it.

Elbert Hubbard

There is no failure except in no longer trying.

Elbert Hubbard

Ninety-nine percent of success is built on former failure.

Charles Kettering

The only time you mustn't fail is the last time you try.

Charles Kettering

Failure is the foundation of success, and the means by which it is achieved.

Lao-tsze

Never give a man up until he has failed at something he likes.

Lewis E. Lawes

Failure is often that early morning hour of darkness which precedes the dawning of the day of success.

Leigh Mitchell

Lack of willpower has caused more failure than lack of intelligence or ability.

Flower A. Newhouse

Failure is not our only punishment for laziness: there is also the success of others.

Jules Renard

Failures are divided into two classes—those who thought and never did, and those who did and never thought.

John Charles Salak

When I was a young man I observed that nine out of ten things I did were failure. I didn't want to be a failure, so I did ten times more work.

George Bernard Shaw

We often discover what will do by finding out what will not do; and probably he who never made a mistake never made a discovery.

Samuel Smiles

He who never fails will never grow rich.
Charles H. Spurgeon

Failure is more frequently from want of energy than want of capital.
Daniel Webster

Formula for failure: Try to please everybody.
Herbert Bayard Swope

~ **Future** ~

All our yesterdays are summarized in our now, and all the tomorrows are ours to shape.
Hal Borland

He that would know what shall be must consider what hath been.
Thomas Fuller

Study the past if you would divine the future.
Confucius

If you do not think about the future, you cannot have one.
John Glasworthy

Who heeds not the future will find sorrow close at hand.
Confucius

Only he who keeps his eye fixed on the far horizon will find his right road.
Dag Hammarskjöld

The executive of the future will be rated by his ability to anticipate his problems rather than to meet them as they come.
Howard Coonley

I hold that man is in the right who is most closely in league with the future.
Henrik Ibsen

It is easy to see, hard to foresee.
Benjamin Franklin

Yesterday is not ours to recover, but tomorrow is ours to win or lose.
Lyndon B. Johnson

The future is purchased by the present.

Samuel Johnson

The future is not in the hands of fate but in ours.

Jules Jusserand

The present is big with the future.

Baron Gottfried Wilhelm von Leibnitz

It's not enough to have a vision of the future, you must also insist on your business operating in accordance with that view.

Frank Lorenzo

Take your hats off to the past, but take your coats off to the future.

Clare Booth Luce

Business more than any other occupation is a continual dealing with the future; it is a continual calculation, an instinctive exercise in foresight.

Henry R. Luce

The most reliable way to anticipate the future is by understanding the present.

John Naisbitt

What will be, is.

Austin O'Malley

The shape of things to come.

H.G. Wells

Every man of us has all the centuries in him.

J. Kenfield Morley

∽ Genius ∾

Mainly an affair of energy.

Matthew Arnold

Perseverance in disguise.

Henry Austin

The transcendent capacity of taking trouble.

Thomas Carlyle

Genius is the ability to reduce the complicated to the simple.

C. W. Ceram

Genius is fostered by industry.

Cicero

Genius is one percent inspiration and ninety-nine percent perspiration.

Thomas Alva Edison

Genius is the ability to put into effect what is in your mind.

F. Scott Fitzgerald

It is the great triumph of genius to make the common appear novel.

Johann Wolfgang von Goethe

The fruit of labor and thought.

Alexander Hamilton

Genius is initiative on fire.

Holbrook Jackson

The faculty of perceiving in an unhabitual way.

William James

The principal mark of genius is not perfection but originality, the opening of new frontiers.

Arthur Koestler

Towering genius disdains a beaten path. It seeks regions hitherto unexplored.

Abraham Lincoln

Genius is infinite painstaking.

Michelangelo

Something not seen with the eyes, but with the mind.

Blaise Pascal

Give your genius a chance.

Persius

An infinite capacity for taking life by the scruff of the neck.

Christopher Quill

Genius only comes to the man who understands with his eyes and his brain.

Auguste Rodin

Genius is only a superior power of seeing.

John Ruskin

Genius is essentially creative; it bears the stamp of the individual who possesses it.

Madame de Staël

Genius seems to be the faculty of having faith in everything, and especially one's self.

Arthur Stringer

∾ Goals ∾

If you cry "forward" you must without fail make plain in what direction to go.

Anton Chekhov

Deviate an inch, lose a thousand miles.

Chinese Proverb

If thou follow thy star, thou can not fail of a glorious haven.

Dante Alighieri

The person who makes a success of living is the one who sees his goal steadily and aims at it unswervingly.

Cecil B. DeMille

Arriving at one goal is the starting point to another.

John Dewey

Knowing what your goal is and desiring to reach it doesn't bring us closer to it. Doing something does.

George Eld

The first two letters of the word goal spell GO.

George Eld

Concentrate on finding your goal, then concentrate on reaching it.

Michael Friedsam

What is the use of running when we are not on the right road?

German Proverb

There is a joy in the pursuit of anything.

Robert Henri

The greatest thing in this world is not so much where we are, but in what direction we are moving.

Oliver Wendell Holmes, Sr.

The riders in a race do not stop short when they reach the goal.

Oliver Wendell Holmes, Sr.

If you can see yourself in possession of your goal, it's half yours.

Tom Hopkins

The world turns aside to let any man pass who knows whither he is going.

David S. Jordan

If your goals are clear, you can achieve them without fuss.

Lao-tzu

Go as far as you can see, and when you get there you will see farther.

Orison Sweet Marden

The basic building block of management is goal setting.

Tom Monaghan

No wind serves him who addresses his voyage to no certain port.

Montaigne

Pride is the product of accomplishing challenging objectives.

William Ouchi

If you don't know where you are going, you will probably end up somewhere else.

Laurence J. Peter

Do not turn back when you are just at the goal.

Publilius Syrus

Keep your eyes on the stars, and your feet on the ground.

Theodore Roosevelt

When a man does not know what harbor he is making for, no wind is the right wind.

Seneca

I aim very high, and then I just keep pushing and pushing and pushing to get what I'm after.

Donald Trump

∽ Government ∽

The primary aim of all government regulation of the economic life of the community should be not to supplant the system of private economic enterprise, but to make it work.

Carl Becker

The marvel of all history is the patience with which men and women submit to burdens unnecessarily laid upon them by governments.

William H. Borah

Public extravagance begets extravagance.

Grover Cleveland

Nothing is easier than spending public money. It does not appear to belong to anybody. The temptation is overwhelming to bestow it on somebody.

Calvin Coolidge

A state is better governed which has but few laws, and those laws strictly observed.

René Descartes

When government goes into business it can always shift its losses to the taxpayer. The government never really goes into business, for it never makes ends meet, and that is the first requisite of business.

Thomas Alva Edison

The only things which are wrong about our government are the things which are wrong with you and me.

Douglas L. Edmonds

A government that is big enough to give you all you want is big enough to take it all away.

Barry Goldwater

If men were angels, no government would be necessary.

Alexander Hamilton

Every time the government attempts to handle our affairs, it costs more and the results are worse than if we had handled them ourselves.

Thomas Jefferson

The less government, the better.

Thomas Jefferson

Govern a great nation as you would cook a small fish. Don't overdo it.

Lao-tsze

We surveyed our (chamber of commerce) members as to what's troubling them. Number one is government. Number two is government. Number three is government, and number four is government.

Richard L. Lesher

In all that the people can individually do well for themselves, government ought not to interfere.

Abraham Lincoln

Every country has the government it deserves.

Joseph de Maistre

The whole duty of government is to prevent crime and to preserve contracts.

William Lamb, Viscount Melbourne

The power of the state is measured by the power that men surrender to it.

Felix Morley

The government can destroy wealth but it cannot create wealth, which is the product of labor and management working with creation.

"Alfalfa Bill" Murray

There's a place for businessmen in politics and that place is right out in the open, saying what you believe.

T. Boone Pickens, Jr.

Government is like a baby—an alimentry canal with a big appetite at one end and no sense of responsibility at the other.

Ronald Reagan

Government—Federal and
State and Local—costs too
much.

Franklin D. Roosevelt

There is a myth that government can do the job cheaply because it doesn't have to make a
profit.

Emanuel S. Savas

As soon as government management begins it upsets the
natural equilibrium of industrial relations, and each interference only requires further bu-
reaucratic control until the end
is the tyranny of the totalitarian
state.

Adam Smith

My reading of history con-
vinces me that most bad government has grown out of too
much government.

John Sharp William

∾ Greatness ⌒

No great thing is created suddenly.

Epictetus

The first virtue of all really
great men is that they are sincere.

Anatole France

Few great men could pass Personnel.

Paul Goodman

No really great man ever
thought himself so.

William Hazlitt

No man was ever great by imitation.

Samuel Johnson

The great man is he who has
not lost the heart of a child.

Mencius

Do not despise the bottom
rungs in the ascent to greatness.

Publilius Syrus

Each of us is great insofar as
we perceive and act on the infinite possibilities which lie un-
discovered and unrecognized
about us.

James Harvey Robinson

The loftiest edifices need the deepest foundations.

George Santayana

The great man is the man who does a thing for the first time.

Alexander Smith

∽ **Growth** ∽

There is no growth except in the fulfillment of obligations.

Anonymous

Give a man opportunity and responsibility, and he will grow.

Louis D. Brandeis

Man was made to grow, not stop.

Robert Browning

Be not afraid of growing slowly, be afraid only of standing still.

Chinese Proverb

All that is human must retrograde if it does not advance.

Edward Gibbon

The key to growth is quite simple: creative men with money.

George Gilder

Who does not increase, decreases.

Hillel

To be a giant and not a dwarf in your profession, you must always be growing.

William Mathews

He who would learn to fly one day must learn to stand and walk and run and climb and dance: one cannot fly into flying.

Friedrich Wilhelm Nietzsche

Undertake something that is difficult; it will do you good. Unless you try to do something beyond what you have already mastered, you will never grow.

Ronald E. Osborn

The keener the want, the lustier the growth.

Wendell Phillips

There is no fruit which is not bitter before it is ripe.

Publilius Syrus

If you want to be a big company tomorrow, you have to start acting like one today.

Thomas Watson

Next to the originator of a good sentence is the first quoter of it.

Ralph Waldo Emerson

∾ **Happiness** ∽

Happiness depends upon ourselves.

Aristotle

There is no happiness except in the realization that we have accomplished something.

Henry Ford, Sr.

Happiness is a habit—cultivate it.

Elbert Hubbard

I am happy and content because I think I am.

Alain René Lesage

Man needs, for his happiness, not only the enjoyment of this or that, but hope and enterprise and change.

Bertrand Russell

We live in an ascending scale when we live happily, one thing leading to another in an endless series.

Robert Louis Stevenson

I find my joy of living in the fierce and ruthless battles of life.

August Strindberg

Haste

One of the great disadvantages of hurry is that it takes such a long time.

Gilbert Keith Chesterton

Desire to have things done quickly prevents their being done thoroughly.

Confucius

Never lose your presence of mind, and never get hurried.

Ralph Waldo Emerson

Nothing can be done at once hastily and prudently.

Publilius Syrus

Whatever is produced in haste goes hastily to waste.

Sa'Di

Too swift arrives as tardy as too slow.

William Shakespeare

Wisely, and slow. They stumble that run fast.

William Shakespeare

Hurry, hurry has no blessing.

Swahili Proverb

Hiring

Hiring is a manager's most important job.

Peter F. Drucker

Making the right people decisions is the ultimate means of controlling an organization.

Peter F. Drucker

Eagles don't flock. You have to find them one at a time.

H. Ross Perot

I am always looking for people who can do a job better than I can.

T. Boone Pickens, Jr.

My philosophy is always to hire the best from the best.

Donald Trump

Hire people who are smarter than you are.

Lew Wasserman

∾ Honesty ∽

An honest man's word is as good as his bond.

Miguel de Cervantes

There is no twilight zone of honesty in business—a thing is right or it's wrong.

John F. Dodge

A show of honesty is in any profession or business the surest way of growing rich.

Jean de La Bruyère

We are never so easily deceived as when we imagine we are deceiving others.

François, Duc de La Rochefoucauld

If honesty did not exist, we ought to invent it as the best means of getting rich.

Honoré Gabriel Riquestti, Comte de Mirabeau

∾ Humor ∽

You grow up the day you have the first real laugh—at yourself.

Ethel Barrymore

A little levity will save many a good heavy thing from sinking.

Samuel Butler

A laugh is worth a hundred groans in any market.

Charles Lamb

The sense of humor is the oil of life's engine. Without it the machinery creaks and groans.

George S. Merriam

Stronger than an army is a quotation whose time has come.

W. I. E. Gates

～ Ideas ～

An idea not capable of realization is an empty soap-bubble.

Benjamin L. Averbach

Your most brilliant ideas come in a flash, but the flash comes only after a lot of hard work.

Edward Blakeslee

The more an idea is developed, the more concise becomes its expression; the more a tree is pruned, the better is the fruit.

Alfred Bougeart

The good ideas are all hammered out in agony by individuals, not spewed out by groups.

Charles Brower

Money never starts an idea; it is the idea that starts the money.

William J. Cameron

Ideas are the mightiest influence on earth. One great thought breathed into a man may regenerate him.

William Ellery Channing

I am more of a sponge than an inventor. I absorb ideas from every source. My principal business is giving commercial value to the brilliant but misdirected ideas of others.

Thomas Alva Edison

Men are strong only so long as
they represent a strong idea.

Sigmund Freud

An idea is a feat of association.

Robert Frost

If you want employees to think
of good ideas, give them good
information.

Mark Gill

Daring ideas are like chessmen
moved forward; they may be
beaten, but they may start a
winning game.

Johann Wolfgang von Goethe

It is not at all likely that anyone ever had a totally original
idea. He may put together old
ideas into a new combination,
but the elements which made
up the new combination were
mostly acquired from other people.

George Grier

The profit of great ideas comes
when you turn them into reality.

Tom Hopkins

Greater than the tread of
mighty armies is an idea whose
time has come.

Victor Hugo

Ideas are, in truth, forces. Infinite, too, is the power of personality. A union of the two always makes history.

Henry James

Ideas lose themselves as quickly
as quail, and one must wing
them the minute they rise out
of the grass—or they are gone.

Thomas F. Kennedy

So long as new ideas are created, sales will continue to
reach new highs.

Charles Kettering

Ideas shape the course of history.

John Maynard Keynes

I could not sleep when I got on
a hunt for an idea, until I had
caught it; and when I thought I
had got it I was not satisfied
until I had repeated it over and
over again, until I had put it in
language plain enough as I
thought, for any boy I knew to
comprehend.

Abraham Lincoln

If you are possessed by an idea,
you find it expressed everywhere, you even smell it.

Thomas Mann

It is the essence of genius to make use of the simplest ideas.

Charles Peguy

Ideas are a capital that bears interest only in the hands of talent.

Antoine de Rivarol

On the clarity of your ideas depends the scope of your success in any endeavor.

James Robertson

If you can't write it down, you don't have an idea.

Andy Rooney

The new idea either finds a champion or dies.

Edward Schon

The most powerful factors in the world are clear ideas in the minds of energetic men of good will.

J. Arthur Thompson

The man with a new idea is a crank—until the idea succeeds.

Mark Twain

Our best ideas come from clerks and stockboys.

Sam Walton

Ideas won't keep. Something must be done about them.

Alfred North Whitehead

∾ Imagination ⇔

What is now proved was once only imagined.

William Blake

Imagination is the living power and prime agent of all human perception.

Samuel Taylor Coleridge

Your imagination pictures beauty, success, desired results. On the other hand, it brings into focus ugliness, distress, and failure. It is for you to decide how you want your imagination to serve you.

Philip Conley

Imagination, not invention, is the supreme master of art as of life.

Joseph Conrad

Every great advance in science has issued from a new audacity of imagination.

John Dewey

(Something) more important than knowledge.

Albert Einstein

There are no days in life so memorable as those which vibrated to some stroke of imagination.

Ralph Waldo Emerson

The first of our senses which we should take care never to let rust through disuse is that sixth sense, the imagination.

Christopher Fry

To develop imaginative powers, we must specialize in our own fields but be alert to new ideas from any source and continually seize and set down our inspirational flashes when they come to us. The longer our imagination retains the idea, the clearer and more attainable it becomes.

Carl Holmes

What the imagination seizes must be truth.

John Keats

Imagination rules the world.

Napoleon I

Imagination is the beginning of creation.

George Bernard Shaw

This world is but canvas to our imaginations.

Henry David Thoreau

～ **Improvement** ～

The biggest room in the world is the room for improvement.

Anonymous

None will improve your lot, if you yourselves do not.

Bertolt Brecht

To face tomorrow with the thought of using the methods of yesterday is to envision life at a standstill. To keep ahead, each one of us, no matter what our task, must search for new and better methods—for even that which we now do well must be done better tomorrow.

James F. Bell

There is only one way to improve one's work—love it.

Phillips Brooks

He may be considered to have a real desire for improvement who daily recognizes his deficiencies, and at the end of each month does not forget what he has learnt.

Tzu Hsia

No matter how small and unimportant what we're doing may seem, if we do it well, it may soon become the step that will lead us to better things.

Channing Pollock

~ Individuality ~

Dare to be what you are and to believe in your own individuality.

Henri Amiel

Don't be a carbon copy of someone else—make your own impression.

Anonymous

If I shall be like him, who will like me?

Anonymous

Resolve to be thyself.

Matthew Arnold

If there is any miracle in the world, any mystery, it is individuality.

Leo Baeck

In order to be irreplaceable one must always be different.

Coco Chanel

Every man has his own organic gift of disposition, faculty, and ability.

James Clarke

Insist on yourself; never imitate.

Ralph Waldo Emerson

Do not wish to be anything but what you are, and try to be that perfectly.

Saint Francis de Sales

Be what you are. This is the first step toward becoming better than you are.

Julius Charles Hare

No man was ever great by imitation.

Samuel Johnson

Beaten paths are for beaten men.

Eric Johnston

It is an absolute perfection to get the very most out of one's own individuality.

Montaigne

All great companies have been built by individuals.

Rupert Murdoch

The mind of each man is as unique as his face.

Talmud

∾ **Industry** ∾

In the ordinary business of life, industry can do anything which genius can do, and very many things which it cannot.

Henry Ward Beecher

Industry is the soul of business and the keystone of prosperity.

Charles Dickens

Everything comes to him who hustles while he waits.

Thomas Alva Edison

Industry need not wish.

Benjamin Franklin

In every rank, both great and small, it is industry that supports us all.

John Gay

Either I will find a way, or I will make one.

Phillip Sidney

Not doing more than the average is what keep the average down.

William Winans

∽ **Information** ∾

A great part of the information I have was acquired by looking up something and finding something else on the way.

Franklin P. Adams

Foolish are the generals who ignore the daily intelligence from the trenches.

Anonymous

Knowledge is power, information is the source of knowledge.

Anonymous

The strategic resource is information.

Daniel Bell

More erroneous conclusions are due to lack of information than to errors of judgment.

Louis D. Brandeis

I am greedy of getting information.

Callimachus

Too often we forget that genius, too, depends upon the data within reach, that even Archimedes could not have devised Edison's inventions.

Ernest Dimnet

Information: The greatest weapon.

Victor Kiam

A businessman's judgment is no better than his information.

Robert P. Lamont

Information, the great equalizer.

John Naisbitt

The new source of power is not money in the hands of a few but information in the hands of many.

John Naisbitt

∽ **Initiative** ∾

Doing the opposite of what you are asked to do doesn't necessarily mean that you are showing initiative.

Anonymous

None will improve your lot, if you yourselves do not.

Bertolt Brecht

If there is no wind, row.

Latin Proverb

Initiative consists of doing the right thing without being told.

Irving Mack

Initiative is a necessary quality for anyone who aspires to rise above the crowd clustered at the foot of the ladder of success; it is characteristic of all true leaders.

Boyd Lindop

Go and wake up your luck.

Persian Proverb

If you don't crack the shell, you can't eat the nut.

Russian Proverb

～ **Innovation** ～

If a man makes a better mousetrap than his neighbor, the world will make a beaten path to his door.

Ralph Waldo Emerson

We are not here to do what has already been done.

Robert Henri

Even when I was young I suspected that much might be done in a better way.

Henry Ford, Sr.

Take an object. Do something to it. Do something else to it.

Jasper Johns

We must not be hampered by yesterday's myths in concentrating on today's needs.

Harold S. Geneen

Not alone for the blade was the bright steel made, and he fashioned the first plowshare.

Charles Mackay

It is always safe to assume, not that the old way is wrong, but that there may be a better way.

Henry R. Harrower

We must assume that there is probably a better way to do almost everything.

Donald M. Nelson

you can see what the next inno-
vation needs to be. When
you're behind, you have to
spend your energy catching up.
Robert Noyce

Take something common and
make it uncommon.
John D. Rockefeller, Sr.

∾ **Inspiration** ᴄᴏ

You have to get your inspiration somewhere, and usually
you get it from reading something else.
Chester Carlson

My role is to be the ultimate in-
spirer, to dream the ultimate
dreams, to see the vision, and
to impart that vision to others.
Arnold C. Greenberg

The great composer does not
set to work because he is inspired, but becomes inspired because he is working.
Ernest Newman

If you wait for inspiration
you'll be standing on the corner after the parade is a mile
down the street.
Ben Nicholas

Just as appetite comes by eat-
ing, so work brings inspiration.
Igor Stravinsky

If the world is cold, make it
your business to build fires.
Horace Traubel

∾ **Instinct** ᴄᴏ

Instinct is untaught ability.
Alexander Bain

Trust the instinct to the end,
though you can render no reason.
Ralph Waldo Emerson

The nose of the mind.
Emile de Girardin

Systems die; instincts remain.
Oliver Wendell Holmes, Jr.

We need not instincts but our own.
Jean de La Fontaine

Be a good animal, true to your animal instincts.
D.H. Lawrence

Well-bred instinct meets reason half-way.
George Santayana

Swift instinct leaps, slow reason feebly climbs.
Edward Young

∽ Intelligence ∾

A man who arrives at an end by the shortest route.
Henri Frédéric Amiel

It is not enough to have a good mind; the main thing is to use it well.
René Descartes

To perceive things in the germ is intelligence.
Lao-tsze

A really intelligent man feels what other men only know.
Montesquieu

The mark of intelligence is to pursue to the end what you have started.
Panchatantra

Intelligence is the effort to do the best you can at your particular job; the quality that gives dignity to that job, whether it happens to be scrubbing a floor or running a corporation.
J.C. Penney

Intelligence is quickness in seeing things as they are.
George Santayana

All men see the same objects, but do not equally understand them. Intelligence is the tongue that discerns and tastes them.

Thomas Traherne

Real intelligence is a creative use of knowledge, not merely an accumulation of facts.

D. Kenneth Winnebrenner

❧ Intuition ❧

The supra-logic that cuts out all routine processes of thought and leaps straight from problem to answer.

Robert Graves

Intuition is reason in a hurry.

Holbrook Jackson

Some executives have a sixth sense that tells them, ''Now is the right time to do it.'' You don't get that out of analysis or number-crunching at a computer.

Robert Jensen

Intuition isn't the enemy, but the ally, of reason.

John K. Lagemann

It is the basically insecure CEO who always seeks more information. Confident leaders trust their intuition.

Drew Lewis

Follow your hunches like the ancient navigators followed the stars. The voyage may be lonely, but the stars will take you where you want to go.

David J. Mahoney

A CEO now has to sense intuitively what the public is thinking every minute of the day.

Carl Menk

Analysis paralysis . . . constantly accumulating new information . . . without giving the mind a chance to percolate and come to a conclusion intuitively can delay any important decision until the time for action expires.

Roy Rowan

Intuition will tell the thinking mind where to look next.

Jonas Salk

It is always with excitement that I wake up in the morning wondering what my intuition will toss up to me, like gifts from the sea. I work with it and rely upon it. It's my partner.

Jonas Salk

A man's heart tells him his opportunities better than seven watchmen on a tower.

Ben Sira

Listen to your gut, no matter how good something sounds on paper.

Donald Trump

∾ Investment ∽

More people should learn to tell their dollars where to go instead of asking them where they went.

Roger W. Babson

Put all good eggs in one basket and then watch that basket.

Andrew Carnegie

The best investment is in the tools of one's own trade.

Benjamin Franklin

'Tis money that begets money.

Thomas Fuller

The best investment on earth is earth.

Louis Glickman

Before you invest—investigate

Salmon P. Halle

Never acquire any business that you don't know how to run.

Robert Wood Johnson

Live on half of what you make and invest the rest in land.

Will Rogers

Sometimes your best investments are the ones you don't make.

Donald Trump

A proverb is the child of experience.

English Proverb

ᴄᴏ Judgment ᴄᴏ

Nothing is of greater value in a man than the power of judgment.

Pietro Aretino

Sound judgment, with discernment, is the best of seers.

Euripides

You're never wrong to do the right thing.

Malcolm Forbes

Associate with men of judgment, for judgment is found in conversation, and we make another man's judgment ours by frequenting his company.

Thomas Fuller

Often a dash of judgment is better than a flash of genius.

Howard W. Newton

Exercise your power of judgment as often as you can, for the first rule of good judgment is practice. The functions of your mind, no less than the muscles of your body, receive their strength through repeated use.

John M. Wilson

One cool judgment is worth a thousand hasty councils. The thing to do is to supply light and not heat.

Woodrow Wilson

The fuel for creative thinking comes from thoughts of others, thoughts expressed in words and recorded in books.

Edgar S. Eliman

∾ **Knowledge** ∽

Knowledge is power.

Francis Bacon

It is better to know nothing than to know what ain't so.

Josh Billings

Knowledge is the only instrument of production that is not subject to diminishing returns.

John M. Clark

The essence of knowledge is, having it, to use it.

Confucius

To be conscious that you are ignorant is a great step to knowledge.

Benjamin Disraeli

Knowledge has become the primary industry, the industry that supplies the economy the essential and central resources of production.

Peter F. Drucker

Knowledge leads to wealth.

Eleazer

Our knowledge is the amassed thought and experience of innumerable minds.

Ralph Waldo Emerson

100

Those who know little are wise
to know those who know much.
Malcolm Forbes

An investment in knowledge always pays the best interest.
Benjamin Franklin

Knowledge is a treasure but
practice is the key to it.
Thomas Fuller

Knowledge without sense is
double folly.
Baltasar Gracián

Know or listen to those who
know.
Baltasar Gracián

Power flows to the man who
knows how.
Elbert Hubbard

There is no substitute for accu-
rate knowledge. Know yourself,
know your business, know your
men.
Randall Jacobs

It is the peculiarity of knowledge that those who really
thirst for it always get it.
Richard Jefferies

Knowledge is of two kinds. We
know a subject ourselves, or we
know where we can get information upon it.
Samuel Johnson

Knowledge rests not upon
truth alone, but upon error
also.
Carl Gustav Jung

Not to know is bad; not to
wish to know is worse.
Nigerian Proverb

Whoever acquires knowledge
but does not practice it is as
one who ploughs but does not
sow.
Sa'Di

When a man's knowledge is
not in order, the more of it he
has the greater will be his confusion.
Herbert Spencer

The desire to knowledge, like
the thirst of riches, increases
ever with the acquisition of it.
Laurence Sterne

No man was ever so completely skilled in the
conduct of life as not to receive new information
from age and experience.

Terence

∾ **Labor** ∽

Men are more important than
tools. If you don't believe so,
put a good tool into the hands
of a poor workman.

John J. Bernet

A man is not idle because he is
absorbed in thought. There is a
visible labor and there is an invisible labor.

Victor Hugo

Labor disgraces no man; unfor-
tunately you occasionally find
men disgrace labor.

Ulysses S. Grant

The bad workmen are decid-
edly of the opinion that bad
workmen ought to receive the
same wages as the good.

John Stuart Mill

The dignity of labor depends
not on what you do, but how
you do it.

Edwin Osgood Grover

And all labor without any play,
boys, makes Jack a dull boy in
the end.

H. A. Page

Men are made stronger on realization that the helping hand
they need is at the end of their
own right arm.

Sidney J. Phillips

I believe in the dignity of labor,
whether with head or hand;
that the world owes no man a
living but that it owes every
man an opportunity to make a
living.

John D. Rockefeller, Jr.

∼ Law ∽

There is no magic in parch-
ment or in wax.

William Henry Ashurst

That law may be set down as
good which is certain in meaning, just in precept, convenient
in execution, agreeable to the
form of government, and productive of virtue in those that
live under it.

Francis Bacon

If you laid all our laws end to
end, there would be no end.

Arthur Baer

In the whole history of law and
order the longest step forward
was taken by primitive man
when, as if by common con-
sent, the tribe sat down in a circle and allowed only one man
to speak at a time.

Curtis Bok

Bad laws are the worst sort of
tyranny.

Edmund Burke

In law, nothing is certain but
the expense.

Samuel Butler

Agree, for the law is costly.

William Camden

Laws should be like clothes.
They should be made to fit the
people they are meant to serve.

Clarence Darrow

The law's made to take care o'
raskills.

George Eliot

If there isn't a law there will be.

Harold Farber

A countryman between two
lawyers is like a fish between
two cats.

Benjamin Franklin

Law cannot persuade where it
cannot punish.

Thomas Fuller

I know no method to secure the
repeal of bad or obnoxious laws
so effective as their stringent execution.

Ulysses S. Grant

How could a state be governed
if every individual remained
free to obey or not to obey the
law according to his private
opinion.

Thomas Hobbes

Laws that do not embody public opinion can never be en-
forced.

Elbert Hubbard

For law is meaningless if there
is no public will to observe it.

Hubert Humphrey

Most business problems require
common sense rather than legal
reference. They require good
judgment and honesty of purpose rather than reference to
the courts.

Edward N. Hurley

The execution of the laws is
more important than the making of them.

Thomas Jefferson

The greater the number of stat-
ues, the greater the number of
thieves and brigands.

Lao-tzse

Discourage litigation. Persuade
your neighbors to compromise
whenever you can.

Abraham Lincoln

Someone has tabulated that we
have 35 million laws on the
books to enforce the ten com-
mandments.

Bert Masterson

The purpose is to prevent the
strong always having their way.

Ovid

We don't need more laws ham-
stringing honest investors and
stockholders. What we do need
is vigorous enforcement of the
existing rules.

T. Boone Pickens, Jr.

Where law ends, there tyranny
begins.

William Pitt

Living for our country entails
respect for and compliance with
the laws, whether we like them
or not, knowing well that a majority of us can change them if
we wish.

Dave E. Smalley

∼ Leadership ∽

True leadership is the art of changing a group from what it is into what it ought to be.

Virginia Allan

The man who cannot control himself becomes absurd when he wants to rule over others.

Isaac Arama

They should rule who are able to rule best.

Aristotle

Anyone who critically analyzes a business learns this: that success or failure of an enterprise depends usually upon one man.

Louis D. Brandeis

Show me a country, a company, or an organization that is doing well and I'll show you a good leader.

Joseph E. Brooks

Govern thyself, and you will be able to govern the world.

Chinese Proverb

It is reassuring for people to feel they have a boss, someone who knows the answers and has charted the course.

George Cukor

The man who follows the crowd will never be followed by a crowd.

Richard S. Donnell

In the simplest terms, a leader is one who knows where he wants to go, gets up, and goes.

John Erskine

The question: "Who ought to be boss?" is like saying "Who ought to be the tenor in the quartet?" Obviously, the man who can sing tenor.

Henry Ford, Sr.

I don't believe in just ordering people to do things. You have to sort of grab an oar and row with them.

Harold S. Geneen

The ability to recognize a problem before it becomes an emergency.

Arnold H. Glasow

A multitude of rulers is not a good thing. Let there be one ruler, one king.

Homer

One who breaks new paths into unfamiliar territory.

Gerald W. Johnson

A leader is best when people barely know that he exists. When his work is done, his aim fulfilled, they will all say, "We did it ourselves."

Lao-tsu

By staying present and aware of what is happening, the leader can do less yet achieve more.

Lao-tsu

The leader knows that constant interventions will block the group's process.

Lao-tsu

Being a general calls for different talents from being a soldier.

Livy

He that would govern others, first should be master of himself.

Philip Massinger

The executive exists to make sensible exceptions to general rules.

Elting E. Morison

Leadership involves finding a parade and getting in front of it.

John Naisbitt

The new leader is a facilitator, not an order giver.

John Naisbitt

A leader is a dealer in hope.

Napoleon I

The inevitable end of multiple chiefs is that they fade and disappear for lack of unity.

Napoleon I

A ship, to run a straight course, can have but one pilot and one steering wheel. The same applies to the successful operation of a business. There cannot be a steering wheel at every seat in an organization.

Jules Ormont

Leadership is the art of getting others to want to do something you are convinced should be done.

Vance Packard

The best leaders are those most interested in surrounding themselves with assistants and associates smarter than they are—being frank in admitting this—and willing to pay for such talents.

Amos Parrish

That man is great who can use the brains of others to carry out his work.

Donn Piatt

Regardless of how you analyze it—whether ethics, market share, labor relations, or profits—it all goes back to the top.

T. Boone Pickens, Jr.

A gifted leader is one who is capable of touching your heart.

J. S. Potofsky

The best executive is the one who has sense enough to pick good men to do what he wants done, and self-restraint enough to keep from meddling with them while they do it.

Theodore Roosevelt

Without a shepherd, sheep are not a flock.

Russian Proverb

Power belongs to the self-possessed.

Louis Antoine Saint-Just

The climax of leadership is to know when to do what.

John R. Scotford

They that govern the most make the least noise.

John Selden

The greatest engineering is the engineering of men.

Robert Louis Stevenson

The ability to handle uncertainty.

David A. Thomas

The outstanding leaders of every age are those who set up their own quotas and constantly exceed them.

Thomas Watson

The commander cannot shoot side by side with his soldier— he must retain perspective.

David Wolffsohn

∽ Learning ∾

They know enough who know how to learn.

Henry Adams

Don't learn the tricks of the trade—learn the trade.

Anonymous

Ask and learn.

Apocrypha

A free curiosity has more efficacy in learning than a frightful enforcement.

Saint Augustine

Man can learn nothing unless he proceeds from the known to the unknown.

Claude Bernard

The eagle never lost so much time as when he submitted to learn from the crow.

William Blake

Do not fail to be a novice in the beginning, because all doing comes from learning.

Erskine Caldwell

Get over the idea that only children should spend their time in study. Be a student so long as you still have something to learn, and this will mean all your life.

Henry L. Doherty

Learning—learning—learning that is the secret.

Ahad Ha'am

Man is an imitative animal. This quality is the germ of all education in him. From his cradle to his grave he is learning to do what he sees others do.

Thomas Jefferson

Learn the art of learning, and you are well on the way to achievement.

Grenville Kleiser

A prudent man should always follow in the path trodden by great men and imitate those who are most excellent.

Nicolò Machiavelli

What we learn with pleasure we never forget.

Louis Mercier

It is good to rub and polish our brain against that of others.

Montaigne

To relax the mind is to lose it.

Musonius

It is no profit to have learned well, if you neglect to do well.

Publilius Syrus

You should keep on learning as long as there is something you do not know.

Seneca

Learning must be sought; it will not come of itself.

Simeon

If you understand the why and wherefore of what you learn, you do not forget it quickly.

Talmud

To be fond of learning is to be near to knowledge.

Tze-Sze

Like any other artist you must learn your craft—then you can add all the genius you like.

Philip Whitney

∾ **Limitations** ∾

All of us have imagined limitations, but we have also the privilege of pushing them aside, and spreading our lives out.

George Adams

One cannot manage too many affairs; like pumpkins in water, one pops up while you try to hold down the other.

Chinese Proverb

We can't be everything to all people.

Bob Fluor

He that is everywhere is nowhere.

Thomas Fuller

He who begins many things finishes but a few.

Italian Proverb

There are no limitations in what you can do except the limitations of your own mind as to what you cannot do. Don't think you cannot. Think you can.

Darwin P. Kingsley

Know and recognize your limits and attain maximum achievement within them.

Stirling Moss

We are limited only because we believe we are limited.

Oriental Mystical Saying

One cannot, as the Americans say, play every instrument in the band.

Elliot Paul

When a man can put a limit on what he will do, he has put a limit on what he can do.

Charles J. Schwab

We cannot all do all things.

Virgil

One should not get overextended. One should think of all kinds of environments when you determine what kind of debt you can carry.

Sanford Weill

∾ Listening ∾

Nature gave us two ears but
only one tongue so that we
hear twice as much as we speak.

Anonymous

No one is as deaf as the man
who will not listen.

Anonymous

He listens well who takes notes.

Dante Alighieri

To do all the talking and not be
willing to listen is a form of
greed.

Democritus

There are people who instead
of listening to what is being
said to them are already listening to what they are going to
say themselves.

Albert Guinon

A good listener is not only popular everywhere, but after a
while he knows something.

Wilson Mizner

Do more than listen, understand.

John H. Rhoades

Give every man your ear, but
few thy voice.

William Shakespeare

When you talk, you repeat
what you already know; when
you listen, you often learn
something.

Jared Sparks

∾ Luck ∾

I never knew an early-rising,
hardworking, prudent man,
careful of his earnings and
strictly honest, who complained
of bad luck.

Joseph Addison

Fortune helpeth hardy men.

Giovanni Boccaccio

Luck is what you have left over
after you give 100%.

Langston Coleman

Luck is not chance, it's toil.
Fortunes' expensive smile is
earned.

Emily Dickinson

Luck is another name for tenacity of purpose.

Ralph Waldo Emerson

Shallow men believe in luck.
Strong men believe in cause
and effect.

Ralph Waldo Emerson

To men of fortitude is fortune
granted.

Quintas Ennius

Fortune truly helps those who
are of good judgment.

Euripides

There isn't any luck that enters
into anything, unless it's poker
or shooting dice, maybe.

Fred W. Fitch

Diligence is the mother of good
luck.

Benjamin Franklin

A pound of pluck is worth a
ton of luck.

James A. Garfield

I think luck is the sense to recognize an opportunity and the
ability to take advantage of it.

Samuel Goldwyn

What is termed luck usually is
the fruit of shrewdness and per-
sistency.

Baltasar Gracián

I am a great believer in luck,
and I find the harder I work
the more I have of it.

Stephen Leacock

Luck is what happens when
preparation meets opportunity.

Elmer G. Leterman

No victor believes in chance.

Friedrich Wilhelm Nietzsche

Luck means the long nights
you have devoted to work.
Luck means the appointments
you have never failed to keep;
the trains you have never failed
to catch; the hardships and pri-
vations which you have not hes-
itated to endure.

Max O'Rell

Fortune favoureth not the faint-
hearted.

George Pettie

The business that trusts to luck
is a bad business.

Publilius Syrus

Fortune favors the brave.

Terence

He that is afraid of bad luck
will never know good.

Russian Proverb

Chance does nothing that has
not been prepared beforehand.

Alexis de Tocqueville

Chance never helps those who
do not help themselves.

Sophocles

Fortune favors the daring.

Virgil

Neglect not the discourse of the wise.

Ben Sira

⤳ Management ⤳

A good manager arouses enthusiasm.

Mary Kay Ash

A good manager is a man who isn't worried about his own career but rather the careers of those who work for him.

Henry S. M. Burns

Take care of those who work for you and you'll float to greatness on their achievements.

Henry S. M. Burns

The most important thing a manager must do is be certain that the people who report to him know exactly what he expects of them.

Albert V. Casey

Management: Picking men of genius, backing them heavily, and leaving them to direct themselves.

James Bryant Conant

When you find a man who knows his job and is willing to take responsibility, keep out of his way and don't bother him with unnecessary supervision. What you may think is cooperation is nothing but interference.

Thomas Dreier

Management is doing a very few simple things and doing them well.

Peter F. Drucker

113

So much of what we call management consists of making it difficult for people to work.

Peter F. Drucker

If you command wisely, you'll be obeyed cheerfully.

Thomas Fuller

Basically, the problem of management is to produce more goods and services for satisfying people's wants at prices more people can afford to pay.

Paul Garrett

Whenever you are too selfishly looking out for your own interest, you have only one person working for you—yourself. When you help a dozen other people with their problems, you have a dozen people working with you.

William B. Given

What makes these managers strong is that they know how to delegate and how to motivate. They know how to look for the pressure points and how to set priorities. They're the kind of guys who can say: "Forget that, it'll take ten years. Here's what we gotta do now."

Lee Iacocca

The man who gets the most satisfactory results is not always the man with the most brilliant single mind, but rather the man who can best coordinate the brains and talents of his associates.

Walton Jones

I believe that "less is more" in the case of corporate management.

Ray Kroc

Those who give too much attention to trifling things become generally incapable of great ones.

François, Duc de La Rochefoucauld

The greatest administrators do not achieve production through constraints and limitations. They provide opportunities.

Lao-tzu

No man will ever be a big executive who feels that he must, either openly or under cover, follow up every order he gives and sees that it is done—nor will he ever develop a capable assistant.

John Lee Mashin

Never tell people how to do things. Tell them what to do and they will surprise you with their ingenuity.

General George S. Patton

Whatever the quality of a company's assets or business, in the final analysis what counts is management.

Sumner Redstone

Good management consists in showing average people how to do the work of superior people.

John D. Rockefeller, Sr.

We do our best that we know how at the moment, and if it doesn't turn out, we modify it.

Franklin D. Roosevelt

Instead of emulating the autocratic, invincible models of the past, successful managers must lead by inspiring individuals.

John Sculley

The most tragic error of management has been to thoughtlessly assume that the workman is a different sort of person.

Denton K. Swartwout

Management's job is to see the company not as it is, but as it can become.

John W. Teets

A good manager is always profiting more from the people below him than from himself. He recognizes that his source of power within the organization ultimately comes from his subordinates.

Richard Welch

❦ Mistakes

Even brute beasts and wandering birds do not fall into the same traps or nets twice.

Saint Ambrose

Truth will sooner come out of error than from confusion.

Francis Bacon

It is only an error in judgment to make a mistake, but it shows infirmity of character to adhere to it when discovered.

Christian Bovee

Error is the discipline through which we advance.

William Ellery Channing

Any man may make a mistake;
none but a fool will persist in it.

Marcus Tullius Cicero

A man who has committed a
mistake and doesn't correct it is
committing another mistake.

Confucius

Don't ever promote a man who
hasn't made some big mis-
takes—you'll be promoting a
man who hasn't done much.

Herbert H. Dow

Mistakes are often the best
teachers.

James Anthony Froude

Man errs as long as he strives.

Johann Wolfgang von Goethe

History is the study of other
people's mistakes.

Philip Guedalla

The greatest mistake you can
make in life is to be continually
fearing you will make one.

Elbert Hubbard

So far, evolution has been nothing but staggering from one
error to the other.

Henrik Ibsen

Knowledge rests not upon
truth alone, but on error also.

Carl Gustav Jung

To believe it possible we may
be in error is the first step toward getting out of it.

Johann K. Lavater

To avoid all mistakes in the
conduct of great enterprises is
beyond man's powers.

Fabius Maximus

Great men have been character-
ized by the greatness of their
mistakes as well as by the greatness of their achievements.

Abraham Myerson

To make no mistakes is not in
the power of man; but from
their errors and mistakes the
wise and good learn wisdom
for the future.

Plutarch

We make progress if, and only
if, we are prepared to learn
from our mistakes.

Karl R. Popper

The fellow who never makes a
mistake takes his orders from
one who does.

Herbert V. Prochnow

A life spent in making mistakes is not only more honorable but more useful than a life spent doing nothing.

George Bernard Shaw

Probably he who never made a mistake never made a discovery.

Samuel Smiles

Give me the young man who has brains enough to make a fool of himself.

Robert Louis Stevenson

I have learned throughout my life as a composer chiefly through my mistakes and pursuits of false assumptions.

Igor Stravinsky

A man should never be ashamed to own he has been in the wrong, which is but saying, in other words, that he is wiser today than he was yesterday.

Jonathon Swift

Wisdom loves the children of men, but she prefers those who come through foolishness to wisdom.

Paul Tillich

Mistakes are lessons of wisdom. The past cannot be changed. The future is yet in your power.

Hugh White

Error itself may be the happy chance.

Alfred North Whitehead

∾ **Money** ∽

Money talks.

Anonymous

Money makes the man.

Aristodemus

As a man, I should be disgusted if I could not earn plenty of money and the praise of the discriminating.

Arnold Bennett

The happiest time in any man's life is when he is in red-hot pursuit of a dollar with a reasonable prospect of overtaking it.

Josh Billings

Those who have some means think that the most important thing in the world is love. The poor knows that it is money.

Gerald Brenen

Money doesn't always bring happiness. People with ten million dollars are no happier than people with nine million dollars.

Hobart Brown

Yes! Ready money is Aladdin's lamp.

George Noel Gordon, Lord Byron

After all, money, as they say, is miraculous.

Thomas Carlyle

The best foundation in the world is money.

Miguel de Cervantes

Those who despise money will eventually sponge on their friends.

Chinese Proverb

With money you are a dragon; with no money, a worm.

Chinese Proverb

There is no fortress so strong that money cannot take it.

Marcus Tullius Cicero

How pleasant it is to have money!

Arthur Hugh Clough

It is a common observation that any fool can get money; but they are not wise that think so.

Charles Caleb Colton

There is one word, sir, we got from China, that is oftener in the mouths of the American people than any other word in the language. It is Cash, sir, cash!

Frederick Swartout Cozzens

If you have no money, be polite.

Danish Proverb

When a man needs money, he needs money, and not a headache tablet or a prayer.

William Feather

Money not only talks, it screams.

Leslie B. Flynn

Money is like an arm or a leg— use it or lose it.

Henry Ford, Sr.

Remember that money is of a prolific generating nature. Money can beget money, and its offspring can beget more.

Benjamin Franklin

The use of money is all the advantage there is in having money.

Benjamin Franklin

Money in purse will always be in fashion.

Thomas Fuller

The only irreparable mistake in business is to run out of cash. Almost any other mistake in business can be remedied in one way or another. But when you run out of cash, they take you out of the game.

Harold S. Geneen

To have money is to be virtuous, honest, beautiful, and witty. And to be without it is to be ugly and boring and stupid and useless.

Jean Giraudoux

Money is an essential ingredient to happiness in this world.

Alexander Hamilton

The populace may hiss me, but when I go home and think of my money I applaud myself.

Horace

Money swore an oath that nobody that did not love it should ever have it.

Irish Proverb

The principle of commercial nations.

Thomas Jefferson

Even the wisest among men welcome people who bring money more than those who take it away.

Georg Christoph Lichtenberg

Money, if it does not bring you happiness, will at least help you to be miserable in comfort.

Lord Mancroft

When a fellow says it ain't the money but the principle o' the thing, it's the money.

Abe Martin

There's no praise to beat the sort you can put in your pocket.

Molière

You bet I'm out to make a buck. That's the name of the game, isn't it?

Luigino Francesco Paulucci

It is pretty to see what money will do.

Samuel Pepys

Money is to be respected; one of the worst things you can do is handle another person's money without respect for how hard it was to earn.

T. Boone Pickens, Jr.

Money alone sets the world in motion.

Publilius Syrus

When it is a question of money, everybody is of the same religion.

Voltaire

Lack of money is trouble without equal.

François Rabelais

It is not a custom with me to keep money to look at.

George Washington

Beauty is potent, but money is omnipotent.

John Ray

The universal regard for money is one hopeful fact in our civilization.

George Bernard Shaw

When I was young I thought that money was the most important thing in life; now that I am old, I know that it is.

Oscar Wilde

He who has money has in his pocket those who have none.

Leo Tolstoy

With money in your pocket, you are wise and you are handsome and you sing well, too.

Yiddish Proverb

❧   Motivation   ❧

Instead of trying to overcome resistance to what people are not ready to do, find out what they are ready to do.

Anonymous

What you make it to the interest of men to do, that they will do.

Edmund Burke

The number one motivator of people is feedback on results.

Felix "Doc" Blanchard, Jr.

The reward of one duty done is the power to fulfill another.

George Eliot

People most strenuously seek to evaluate their performance by comparing themselves to others, not by using absolute standards.

Leon Festinger

Need and struggle are what excite and inspire us.

William James

Where there is no desire, there will be no industry.

John Locke

Lord, grant that I may always desire more than I can accomplish.

Michelangelo

I want every one of my players to believe that he's the spark that keeps our team moving forward.

Knute Rockne

Recognition for a job well done is high on the list of motivating influences for all people; more important, in many instances, than compensation itself.

John M. Wilson

Scraps from the table of wisdom, that if well-digested yield strong nourishment to thy mind.

Benjamin Franklin

∾ Negativism ∾

"I can't do it" never yet accomplished anything; "I will try" has performed wonders.

George P. Bunham

Any fool can criticize, condemn, and complain—and most fools do.

Dale Carnegie

To believe a business impossible is the way to make it so. How many feasible projects have miscarried through despondency, and been strangled in their birth by a cowardly imagination?

Jeremy Collier

It is the growling man who lives a dog's life.

Coleman Cox

The chronic knocker gets more discomfort from his continual criticism than do all of the people that he is raving against.

Charles J. Dennis

The man who says it can't be done is generally interrupted by someone doing it.

Elbert Hubbard

∽ **Negotiation** ↝

Successful collaborative negotiation lies in finding out what the other side really wants and showing them a way to get it—while you get what you want.

Herb Cohen

He who has learned to disagree without being disagreeable has discovered the most valuable secret of a diplomat.

Robert Estabrook

The ability to see the situation as the other side sees it is one of the most important skills a negotiator can possess.

Roger Fisher

Do you know that the ready concession of minor points is a part of the grace of life.

Henry Harland

Don't ever slam the door; you might want to go back.

Don Herold

Enter into negotiations with the intention of creating an agreement that will allow both parties to achieve their essential goals.

Tom Hopkins

The greater the number of issues that two negotiators can identify, the more room there is to structure an outcome in which both can perceive themselves as winners.

Fred Jandt

The first man to raise his voice has lost the argument.

Japanese Proverb

Always ask for something in return for any concession. Ask: "If I do this, will you do that?" Don't just give in.

Gary Karrass

You cannot antagonize and influence at the same time.

John Knox

When I'm getting ready to reason with a man I spend one-third of my time thinking about myself and what I am going to say—and two-thirds thinking about him and what he is going to say.

Abraham Lincoln

The only successful negotiations are those in which everyone wins.

Jerry Nierenberg

There are two sides to every question.

Protagoras

He who resolves never to ransack any mind but his own will be soon be reduced from mere barrenness to the poorest of all imitations: he will be obliged to imitate himself.

Sir Joshua Reynolds

ᔓ **Obstacles** ᔒ

Courage and perseverance have a magical talisman before which difficulties disappear and obstacles vanish into air.

John Quincy Adams

If you want a place in the sun, you've got to expect a few blisters.

Anonymous

The great pleasure in life is doing what people say you cannot do.

Walter Bagehot

Every noble work is at first impossible.

Thomas Carlyle

It is interesting to notice how some minds seem almost to create themselves, springing up under every disadvantage and working their solitary but irresistible way through a thousand obstacles.

Washington Irving

The greater the obstacle, the more glory in overcoming it.

Molière

The real test in golf and in life is not in keeping out of the rough, but in getting out after we are in.

John H. Moore

Obstacles are those frightful things you see when you take your eyes off the goal.

Hannah More

Life is just one damned thing after another.

Frank Ward O'Malley

There are no disasters in business that you can't avoid—if you see them coming and make the adjustments.

T. Boone Pickens, Jr.

There are moments when everything goes well; don't be frightened, it won't last.

Jules Renard

The difficult we do immediately. The impossible takes a little longer.

Slogan of U.S. Army Services Forces

The crisis of yesterday is the joke of tomorrow.

H. G. Wells

Sometimes it is more important to discover what one cannot do than what one can do.

Lin Yutang

~ Opportunity ~

Make opportunities happen.

Mary Kay Ash

A wise man will make more opportunities than he finds.

Francis Bacon

The best jobs haven't been started. The best work hasn't been done.

Berton Braley

Too many people are thinking of security instead of opportunity. They seem more afraid of life than death.

James F. Byrnes

The sure way to miss success is to miss the opportunity.

Victor Chasles

The reason so many people never get anywhere in life is because, when opportunity knocks, they are out in the backyard looking for four-leaf clovers.

Walter P. Chrysler

Every one has a fair turn to be as great as he pleases.

Jeremy Collier

No great man ever complains of want of opportunity.

Ralph Waldo Emerson

A generation ago there were a thousand men to every opportunity, while today there are a thousand opportunities to every man.

Henry Ford, Sr.

How many times it thundered before Franklin took the hint! How many apples fell on Newton's head before he took the hint!

Robert Frost

God gives the nuts, but he does not crack them.

German Proverb

Let us snatch our opportunity from the day, my friends.

Horace

Many do with opportunities as children do at the seashore; they fill their little hands with sand and let the grains fall through, one by one, till all are gone.

Tom Jones

There is no security on this earth; there is only opportunity.

General Douglas MacArthur

Opportunity has power everywhere: always let your hook be hanging; where you least expect it, there will swim a fish.

Ovid

Every successful business in the world is in existence because its founder recognized in a problem or need an opportunity to be of service to others.

J. Sig Paulson

The universe is full of magical things patiently waiting for our wits to grow sharper.

Eden Phillpotts

The trouble with opportunity is that it always comes disguised as hard work.

Herbert V. Prochnow

While we stop to think, we often miss our opportunity.

Publilius Syrus

So little done, so much to do.
Cecil Rhodes

Everything in the world remains to be done or done over.
Lincoln Steffens

The gates of opportunity and advancement swing on these four hinges: initiative, industry, insight, and integrity.
William Arthur Ward

Opportunities multiply as they are seized; they die when neglected.
John Wicker

∾ Optimism ∾

Without optimism there can be no vitality.
John Buchan

I am glad I am an optimist. The pessimist is half-licked before he starts. The optimist has won half the battle.
Thomas A. Buckner

Optimism is essential to achievement and it is also the foundation of courage and of true progress.
Nicholas M. Butler

I am an optimist. It does not seem too much use being anything else.
Sir Winston Churchill

My center is giving way, my right is pushed back, situation excellent, I am attacking.
Ferdinand Foch

There's a good time coming, boys!
Charles Mackay

A pessimist is one who makes difficulties of his opportunities; an optimist is one who makes opportunities of his difficulties.
Reginald B. Mansell

The hopeful man sees success where others see failure, sunshine where others see shadows and storm.
Orison Sweet Marden

If you count the sunny and the cloudy days of the whole year, you will find that the sunshine predominates.

Ovid

'Twixt the optimist and pessimist the difference is droll: the optimist sees the doughnut but the pessimist sees the hole.

McLandburgh Wilson

∾ Originality ∾

What is originality? It is being one's self, and reporting accurately what we see and are.

Ralph Waldo Emerson

Everything has been thought of before, but the problem is to think of it again.

Johan Wolfgang von Goethe

Originality is simply a pair of fresh eyes.

Thomas W. Higginson

A thought is often original, though you have uttered it a hundred times. It has come to you over a new route, by a new and express train of association.

Oliver Wendell Holmes, Sr.

What is originality? Undetected plagiarism.

Dean William Randolph Inge

Many have original minds who do not think it—they are led away by custom.

John Keats

My guess is that well over 80 percent of the human race goes through life without having a single original thought.

H. L. Mencken

All good things which exist are the fruits of originality.

John Stuart Mill

I invent nothing. I rediscover.

Auguste Rodin

What the world calls originality is only an unaccustomed method of tickling it.

George Bernard Shaw

The great man is the man who does a thing for the first time.

Alexander Smith

Originality is the supreme evidence of genius.

Luc de Clapiers, Marquis de Vauvenargues

Proverbs, the ready money of human experience.

James Russell Lowell

∾ **Partnership** ∽

When two friends have a common purse, one sings and the other weeps.

Anonymous

Those whose ways are different do not make plans together.

Confucius

Choose very, very carefully, because a divorce in business is just as traumatic and expensive as a personal one.

James P. Gore

That which is possessed in common is commonly neglected.

Latin Proverb

One bad general does better than two good ones.

Napoleon I

Two heads are better than one; but this refers only to asparagus.

W. Pett Ridge

A friendship founded on business is better than a business founded on friendship.

John D. Rockefeller, Jr.

The pot that belongs to partners is neither hot nor cold.

Talmud

130

The man who goes alone can start today; but he who travels with another must wait till that other is ready.

Henry David Thoreau

Two captains sink the ship.

Turkish Proverb

∾ **Patience** ∾

Our patience will achieve more than our force.

Edmund Burke

Once you have learned what to unlearn, success will come, so work and wait.

Ronald Hambleton

Patience, and the mulberry leaf becomes a silk gown.

Chinese Proverb

Patience, time, and money accommodate all things.

George Herbert

Patience is the know which secures the seam of victory.

Chinese Proverb

We shall sooner have the fowl by hatching the egg than by smashing it.

Abraham Lincoln

Everything comes to him who hustles while he waits.

Thomas Alva Edison

Success is to know how to wait.

Joseph de Maistre

Patience and application will carry us through.

Thomas Fuller

All things come to him who waits—provided he knows what he is waiting for.

Woodrow Wilson

Perseverance

He overtakes at last who tires not.

Nathan Bailey

Never say die.

Richard H. Barham

With ordinary talent and extraordinary perseverance, all things are attainable.

Thomas F. Buxton

Big shots are only little shots who keep shooting.

Dale Carnegie

Men fail much oftener from want of perseverance than from want of talent.

William Cobbett

Even the woodpecker owes his success to the fact that he uses his head and keeps pecking away until he finishes the job he starts.

Coleman Cox

Who persists in knocking will succeed in entering.

M. Ibn Ezra

Fall seven times, stand up eight.

Japanese Proverb

Great works are performed not by strength but by perseverance.

Samuel Johnson

We can do anything we want to do if we stick to it long enough.

Helen Keller

Many strokes overthrow the tallest oaks.

John Lyly

Victory belongs to the most persevering.

Napoleon I

Let me tell you the secret that has led me to my goal. My strength lies solely in my tenacity.

Louis Pasteur

Some men give up their designs when they have almost reached the goal; while others, on the contrary, obtain a victory by exerting, at the last moment, more vigorous efforts than before.

Polybius

There is nothing which persevering effort cannot overcome.

Seneca

By perseverance the snail
reached the ark.

Charles H. Spurgeon

Don't let the bastards grind
you down.

Joseph W. Stilwell

To endure is greater than to
dare.

William Makepeace Thackeray

Don't bother about genius.
Don't worry about being
clever. Trust to hard work, perseverance and determination.
And the best motto for a long
march is "Don't grumble.
Plug on!"

Sir Frederick Treves

There's such a thing as giving
up too soon. You can always
get one more spoonful of juice
out of a grapefruit.

Milt Weiss

∼ Persistence ∽

It is better never to begin a
good work than, having begun
it, to stop.

Venerable Bede

Again and again, when the
struggle seems hopeless and all
opportunity lost, some man or
woman with a little more courage, a little more effort, brings
victory.

James F. Bell

Energy and persistence conquer
all things.

Benjamin Franklin

Always at it wins the day.

German Proverb

If you add a little to a little and
do this often, soon the little will
become great.

Hesiod

Never despair, keep pushing on!
Thomas Lipton

When nothing seems to help, I
go and look at a stonecutter
hammering away at his rock,
perhaps a hundred times without as much as a crack showing
in it. Yet at the hundred and
first blow it will split in two,
and I know it was not that last
blow that did it, but all that
had gone before.
Jacob A. Riis

It's easy enough to be a starter,
but are you a sticker too? It's
easy enough to begin a job. It's
harder to see it through.
Margaret Thatcher

Did you ever hear of a man
who had striven all his life faith-
fully and singly toward an object, and in no measure ob-
tained it?
Henry David Thoreau

～ **Persuasion** ～

Politeness is better than logic.
You can often persuade when
you cannot convince.
Josh Billings

Charm is a way of getting the
answer yes without having
asked any clear question.
Albert Camus

To please people is a great step
towards persuading them.
*Philip Dormer Stanhope, Earl of
Chesterfield*

He who wants to persuade
should put his trust not in the
right argument, but in the
right word. The power of
sound has always been greater
than the power of sense.
Joseph Conrad

To seduce most anyone, ask for
and listen to his opinion.
Malcolm Forbes

Would you persuade, speak of
interest, not of reason.
Benjamin Franklin

Soft words are hard arguments.
Thomas Fuller

A man's success in business today turns upon his power of getting people to believe he has something that they want.

Gerald Stanley Lee

The very essence of all power to influence lies in getting the other person to participate.

Harry A. Overstreet

People are generally better persuaded by the reasons which they have themselves discovered than by those which have come into the mind of others.

Blaise Pascal

One of the best ways to persuade others is with your ears— by listening to them.

Dean Rusk

I see that everywhere among the race of men it is the tongue that wins.

Sophocles

If you can't convince them, confuse them.

Harry S. Truman

∾ Planning ↶

A pilot who sees from afar will not make his boat a wreck.

Amenemhet I

Plan your work! Work your plan!

Anonymous

We can't cross a bridge until we come to it, but I always like to lay down a position ahead of time.

Bernard M. Baruch

A thought which does not result in action is nothing much, and an action which does not proceed from thought is nothing at all.

Georges Bernanos

Make no little plans; they have no magic to stir men's blood. Make big plans, aim high in hope and work.

Daniel H. Burnham

In life, as in chess, forethought wins.

Charles Buxton

An important key to driving is knowing where the road leads.

Kenneth L. Fisher

A danger foreseen is half avoided.

Thomas Fuller

Act quickly, think slowly.

Greek Proverb

Look ere ye leap.

John Heywood

The great architect of the universe never built a stairway that leads to nowhere.

Robert A. Millikan

Strategic planning is worthless—unless there is first a strategic vision. A strategic vision is a clear image of what you want to achieve, which then organizes and instructs every step toward that goal.

John Naisbitt

If you don't know where you are going, you will probably end up somewhere else.

Laurence J. Peter

Planning is but another word for the vision that sees a creative achievement before it is manifest.

James L. Pierce

Mighty rivers can easily be leaped at their source.

Publilius Syrus

In every enterprise consider where you would come out.

Publilius Syrus

It is a bad plan that admits of no modification.

Publilius Syrus

Plans get you into things, but you've got to work your way out.

Will Rogers

Our plans miscarry because they have no aim. When a man does not know what harbor he is making for, no wind is the right wind.

Seneca

To fear the worst oft cures the worse.

William Shakespeare

Proper planning prevents piss-poor performance.

The Six ''P'' Principle

Only those who get into scrapes with their eyes open can find the safe way out.

Logan P. Smith

An intelligent plan is the first step to success. The man who plans knows where he is going, knows what progress he is making, and has a pretty good idea when he will arrive. Planning is the open road to your destination. If you don't know where you are going, how can you expect to get there?

Basil S. Walsh

Few people plan to fail, they just fail to plan.

Lee Whistler

∽ Positivism ∾

The only barriers to success are mental obstacles.

Clarence Blasier

Positive anything is better than negative nothing.

Elbert Hubbard

We must look for the opportunity in every difficulty instead of being paralyzed at the thought of the difficulty in every opportunity.

Walter E. Cole

Nothing is impossible: There are ways which lead to everything; and if we had sufficient will we should always have sufficient means.

François, Duc de La Rochefoucauld

A single sunbeam is enough to drive away many shadows.

Saint Francis of Assisi

I can complain because rose bushes have thorns or rejoice because thorn bushes have roses. It's all how you look at it.

J. Kenfield Morley

I believe that if you think about disaster, you will get it. Brood about death and you hasten your demise. Think positively and masterfully, with confidence and faith, and life becomes more secure, more fraught with action, richer in achievement and experience.

Edward Rickenbacker

Success comes to the man who grits his teeth, squares his jaw, and says, "There is a way for me and, by jingo, I'll find it."

Clifford Sloan

Negative thoughts can be neutralized only by positive ones.

Clement Stone

Once we become more positive about ourselves, we will be much more successful than we ever dreamed of being.

Lila Swell

They can because they think they can.

Virgil

∾ **Possibilities** ↵

All things are possible until they are proved impossible— and even the impossible may only be so, as of now.

Pearl S. Buck

Few men during their lifetime come anywhere near exhausting the resources dwelling within them. There are deep wells of strength that are never used.

Admiral Richard E. Byrd

The mind of man is capable of anything—because everything is in it, all the past as well as all the future.

Joseph Conrad

Every person is a bundle of possibilities and he is worth what life may get out of him before it is through.

Harry Emerson Fosdick

Possibilities are infinite.

Thomas Fuller

Nothing is unthinkable, nothing impossible to the balanced person, provided it arises out of the needs of life and is dedicated to life's further developments.

Lewis Mumford

One does not know—cannot know—the best that is in one.

Friedrich Wilhelm Nietzsche

The world which credits what is done is cold to all that might have been.

Alfred, Lord Tennyson

∽ Potpourri ↝

The leaders of the French Revolution excited the poor against the rich; this made the rich poor, but it never made the poor rich.

Fisher Ames

Lead, follow, or get out of the way.

Anonymous

All mankind is divided into three classes: Those that are immovable, those that are movable, and those that move.

Arabian Proverb

A generation is a drama with four or five thousand outstanding characters.

Honoré de Balzac

Unless each man produces more than he receives, increases his output, there will be less for him and all the others.

Bernard M. Baruch

The only pretty store is one full of people.

William T. Dillard

Everything that is really great and inspiring is created by the individual who can labor in freedom.

Albert Einstein

Live in terms of your strong points. Magnify them. Let your weaknesses shrivel up and die from lack of nourishment.

William Y. Elliott

Men are all inventors sailing forth on a voyage of discovery.

Ralph Waldo Emerson

Some will always be above others. Destroy the inequality today and it will appear again tomorrow.

Ralph Waldo Emerson

Time and money spent in helping men to do more for themselves is far better than mere giving.

Henry Ford, Sr.

A man who has been the indisputable favorite of his mother keeps for life the feeling of a conqueror, that confidence of success that often induces real success.

Sigmund Freud

Let us live in as small a circle as we will; we are either debtors or creditors before we have had time to look around.

Johann Wolfgang von Goethe

Knowing top leaders pays off if you have problems with bureaucrats.

Armand Hammer

The crab instructs its young, "walk straight ahead—like me."

Hindustani Proverb

A runaway monk never speaks well of his monastery.

Italian Proverb

Your levelers wish to level down as far as themselves. But they cannot bear leveling up to themselves. They would all have some people under them. Why not then have some people above them?

Samuel Johnson

Morale is faith in the man at the top.

Albert S. Johnstone

Continual input obscures genuine insight.

Lao-tzu

With the catching ends the pleasures of the chase.

Abraham Lincoln

The turtle lays thousands of eggs without anyone knowing, but when the hen lays an egg, the whole country is informed.

Malaysian Proverb

Obey that impulse.

Thomas L. Masson

Men are most apt to believe what they least understand.

Montaigne

Never be a bear on the United States.

J. P. Morgan

The time men spend in trying to impress others they could spend in doing the things by which others would be impressed.

Frank Romer

Those who cannot remember the past are condemned to repeat it.

George Santayana

When a man hasn't a good reason for doing a thing, he has a good reason for letting it alone.

Sir Walter Scott

It is energy—the central element of which is will—that produces the miracles of enthusiasm in all ages.

Samuel Smiles

The market will not go up unless it goes up, nor will it go down unless it goes down, and it will stay the same unless it does either.

Adam Smith

You don't buy stock because it has real value. You buy it because you feel there is always a greater fool down the street ready to pay more than you paid.

Donald J. Stocking

There are as many opinions as there are men.

Terence

∾ **Preparation** ∽

If you want to be employed, be employable.

William J. H. Boetcker

The man who is prepared has his battle half fought.

Miguel de Cervantes

Success depends on preparation, and without such preparation there is sure to be failure.

Confucius

Practice yourself in little things.

Epictetus

Responsibility gravitates toward him who gets ready for it.

George Walter Fiske

Before everything else, getting ready is the secret of success.

Henry Ford, Sr.

In the world who does not know how to swim goes to the bottom.

George Herbert

Today is the sure preparation for tomorrow and all the tomorrows that follow.

Harriet Martineau

Fortune favors the prepared mind.

Louis Pasteur

Nothing can be made of nothing; he who has laid up no material can produce no combination.

Sir Joshua Reynolds

To climb steep hills requires slow pace at first.

William Shakespeare

Politics is perhaps the only profession for which no preparation is thought necessary.

Robert Louis Stevenson

Problems

The first step in problem-solving is to admit that a problem exists.

Mary Kay Ash

The only way you're going to solve problems is by communication.

Sir David Attenborough

If things are not going well with you, begin your effort at correcting the situation by carefully examining the service you are rendering, and especially the spirit in which you are rendering it.

Roger W. Babson

When you approach a problem, strip yourself of preconceived opinions and prejudice, assemble and learn the facts of the situation, make the decision which seems to you to be the most honest, and then stick to it.

Chester Bowles

There is no problem of human nature which is insoluble.

Ralph J. Bunche

The biggest problem in the world could have been solved when it was small.

Witter Bynner

A man must be harder than what hits him. Yes, he must be diamond-hard. Then he'll not be "fed-up" with his little personal troubles.

Herbert N. Casson

The prizes go to those who meet emergencies successfully.

William Feather

If something goes wrong, it is more important to talk abut who is going to fix it, than who is to blame.

Francis J. Gable

All problems become smaller if you don't dodge them but confront them. Touch a thistle timidly, and it pricks you; grasp it boldly, and its spine crumbles.

William F. Halsey, Jr.

A good problem statement often includes: (a) what is known, (b) what is unknown, and (c) what is sought.

Edward Hodnett

Problems are only opportunities in work clothes.

Henry J. Kaiser

A problem well stated is a problem half solved.

Charles Kettering

The happy and efficient people in this world are those who accept trouble as a normal detail of human life and resolve to capitalize it when it comes along.

H. Bertram Lewis

In the final analysis, there is no other solution to man's problems but the day's honest work, the day's honest decisions, the day's generous utterance, and the day's good deed.

Clare Booth Luce

No matter how big and tough a problem may be, get rid of confusion by taking one little step towards solution. Do something. Then try again. At the worst, so long as you don't do it the same way twice, you will eventually use up all the wrong ways of doing it and thus the next try will be the right one.

George F. Nordenholt

Think as you work, for in the final analysis your worth to your company comes not only in solving problems but in anticipating them.

Herbert H. Ross

The wise man thinks about his troubles only when there is some purpose in doing so; at other times he thinks about other things.

Bertrand Russell

I never take a problem to bed with me at night.

Harry S. Truman

Never complain about your troubles; they are responsible for more than half of your income.

Robert Updegraff

∽ **Procrastination** ∾

"One of these days" is none of these days.

Anonymous

Often greater risk is involved in postponement than in making a wrong decision.

Harry A. Hopf

Delay always breeds danger and to protract a great design is often to ruin it.

Miguel de Cervantes

Putting off a hard thing makes it impossible.

George H. Lorimer

He who considers too much will perform little.

Johann Friedrich von Schiller

Chi Wen Tzu always thought three times before taking action. Twice would have been quite enough.

Confucius

By-and-by is easily said.

William Shakespeare

What may be done at any time will be done at no time.

Thomas Fuller

Procrastination is the thief of time.

Edward Young

∽ Profit ∾

Business without profit is not business any more than a pickle is a candy.

Charles F. Abbott

We have learned the lesson that when opportunities for profit diminish, opportunities for jobs likewise disappear.

Executive Council, AFL

Profit is a natural by-product of doing something well.

Anonymous

In all things, follow the bounding ball to the right-hand corner of the P&L statement.

Mylle Bell

It is in the interest of the community that a man in a free business, in a competitive business, shall have the incentive to make just as much money as he can.

Louis D. Brandeis

I don't want to do business with those who don't make a profit, because they can't give the best service.

Lee Bristol

It is a socialist idea that making profits is a vice; I consider that the real vice is making losses.

Sir Winston Churchill

Civilization and profits go hand in hand.

Calvin Coolidge

Profitability is the sovereign criterion of the enterprise.

Peter F. Drucker

When shallow critics denounce the profit motive inherent in our system of private enterprise, they ignore the fact that it is an economic support of every human right we possess and without it, all rights would disappear.

Dwight D. Eisenhower

The worst crime against working people is a company which fails to operate at a profit.

Samuel Gompers

The profit system is simply a fair and just reward for effort, and it applies to every executive and every workman.

Ernest Hermann

The smell of profit is clean,
and sweet, whatever the source.

Juvenal

A sale without profit is a sale
without honor.

Paul Kalmanovitz

The engine that drives enterprise is not thrift, but profit.

John Maynard Keynes

Profit is a must. There can be
no security for any employee in
any business that doesn't make
money. There can be no
growth for that business. There
can be no opportunity for the
individual to achieve his personal ambitions unless his company makes money.

Duncan C. Menzies

The successful producer of an
article sells it for more than it
cost him to make, and that's
his profit, but the customer
buys it only because it is worth
more to him than he pays for
it, and that's his profit. No one
can long make a profit producing anything unless the customer makes a profit using it.

Samuel B. Pettengill

Profits in a competitive economy are a measure of effective,
efficient operation and should
be worn as a badge of accom-
plishment and of honor.

Philip D. Reed

Nothing contributes so much to
the prosperity and happiness of
a country as high profits.

David Ricardo

❧ **Progress** ❧

Progress in every age results
only from the fact that there
are some men and women who
refuse to believe that what they
knew to be right cannot be
done.

Russell W. Davenport

Restlessness and discontent are
the first necessities of progress.

Thomas Alva Edison

Progress in industry depends
very largely on the enterprise
of deep-thinking men, who are
ahead of the times in their
ideas.

William Ellis

Nature knows no pause in progress and development, and at-
taches her curse on all inaction.

Johann Wolfgang von Goethe

Very much of what we call the progress of today consists in getting rid of false ideas, false conceptions of things, and in taking a point of view that enables us to see the principles, ideas and things in right relation to each other.

William D. Hoard

You can't sit on the lid of progress. If you do, you will be blown to pieces.

Henry J. Kaiser

Where there is no progress there is disintegration. Today a thousand doors of enterprise are open to you to useful work. Today is the day in which to attempt and achieve something worthwhile.

Grenville Kleiser

To act, that each tomorrow find us farther than today.

Henry Wadsworth Longfellow

Progress has no greater enemy than habit.

José Marti

Whatever there be of progress in life comes not through adaptation but through daring, through obeying the blind urge.

Henry Miller

From tension all human progress springs.

Felix Morley

Business is like a man rowing a boat upstream. He has no choice; he must go ahead or he will go back.

Lewis E. Pierson

The greater part of progress is the desire to progress.

Seneca

The life and spirit of the American economy is progress and expansion.

Harry S. Truman

Progressiveness is looking forward intelligently, looking within critically, and moving on incessantly.

Waldo Pondray Watten

Fundamental progress has to do with the reinterpretation of basic ideas.

Alfred North Whitehead

Panic of error is the death of progress.

Alfred North Whitehead

The art of progress is to preserve order amid change and to preserve change amid order.

Alfred North Whitehead

∾ **Promises** ⋍

Promises may get friends, but it is performance that must nurse and keep them.

Owen Feltham

An acre of performance is worth the whole Land of Promise.

James Howell

Knowing promise to be debt, I will pay it with performance.

John Lyly

Never promise more than you can perform.

Publilius Syrus

∾ **Property** ⋍

Great is the good fortune of a state in which the citizens have a moderate and sufficient property.

Aristotle

The great end for which men entered into society.

William Camden

Upon the sacredness of property civilization itself depends.

Andrew Carnegie

Men honor property above all else; it has the greatest power in human life.

Euripides

Endeavor vigorously to increase your property.

Horace

The instinct of ownership is fundamental in man's nature.

William James

Every man has by nature the right to possess property as his own.

Pope Leo XIII

Property is the fruit of labor; property is desirable; it is a positive good in the world. That some should be rich shows that others may become rich and, hence, is just encouragement to industry and enterprise.

Abraham Lincoln

With us it is not a matter of re-
forming private property, but
of abolishing it.

Karl Marx

It should be remembered that
the foundation of the social con-
tract is property.

Jean Jacques Rousseau

∽ Purpose ∾

The first thing to do in life is to
do with purpose what one pro-
poses to do.

Pablo Casals

Men, like nails, lose their use-
fulness when they lose direction
and begin to bend.

Walter S. Landor

A windmill is eternally at work
to accomplish one end, al-
though it shifts with every vari-
ation of the weathercock, and
assumes ten different positions
in a day.

Charles Caleb Colton

The great and glorious master-
piece of man is to know how to
live to purpose.

Montaigne

The secret to success is constancy to purpose.

Benjamin Disraeli

To forget one's purposes is the
commonest form of stupidity.

Friedrich Wilhelm Nietzsche

Great minds have purposes,
others have wishes.

Washington Irving

He who is fixed to a star does
not change his mind.

Leonardo da Vinci

All good maxims are in the world. We only
need to apply them.

Blaise Pascal

～ **Quality** ～

Anybody can cut prices, but it
takes brains to produce a better
article.

Philip Daniel Armour

Quality isn't something that
can be argued into an article or
promised into it. It must be put
there. If it isn't put there, the
finest sales talk in the world
won't act as a substitute.

Charles G. Campbell

When everything would seem
to be a matter of price, there
lies still at the root of great business success the very much
more important factor of quality.

Andrew Carnegie

Quality is precisely measured
by the oldest, most respected
measurements—cold, hard cash.

Philip Crosby

Styling and value are what sells
cars, but quality is what keeps
them sold.

Lee Iacocca

If I had a brick for every time
I've repeated the phrase
Q.S.C. & V. (Quality, Service,
Cleanliness, and Value) I think
I'd probably be able to bridge
the Atlantic Ocean.

Ray Kroc

Conceal a flaw, and the world will imagine the worst.

Martial

Trifles make perfection, and perfection is no trifle.

Michelangelo

People don't give a hoot about who made the original whatzit. They want to know who makes the best one.

Howard W. Newton

People forget how fast you did a job—but they remember how well you did it.

Howard W. Newton

Quality is never an accident. It is always the result of intelligent effort. There must be the will to produce a superior thing.

John Ruskin

Companies have to improve not only the quality of their products but the quality of the process by which their products are designed and built.

Frank Schrontz

Cheat me in price, but not in the goods I purchase.

Spanish Proverb

Any deviation from design specifications quickly gets expensive in terms of warranty costs and lost goodwill.

Genichi Taguchi

The experience and observation of several ages, gathered and summed up into one expression.

Robert South

∽ **Reason** ∽

Learn to reason forward and backward on both sides of a question.

Thomas Blandi

The bond of society is reason and speech.

Marcus Tullius Cicero

If you will not hear Reason, she will surely rap your knuckles.

Benjamin Franklin

The only thing you've got going for you as a human being is your ability to reason and your common sense. Remember, a horse is stronger and a dog is friendlier.

Lee Iacocca

Pure reason avoids extremes, and requires one to be wise in moderation.

Molière

Most of our so-called reasoning consists in finding arguments for going on believing as we already do.

James Harvey Robinson

Be led by reason.
Solon

Emotion has taught mankind to reason.
Luc de Clapiers, Marquis de Vauvenargues

It is the triumph of reason to get on well with those who possess none.
Voltaire

∽ **Recruitment** ∾

No general can fight his battles alone. He must depend upon his ability to secure the right man for the right place.
J. Ogden Armour

The best resumes don't produce the best people.
Robert Bernstein

The employer generally gets the employees he deserves.
Walter Bilbey

The same man cannot well be skilled in everything; each has his special excellence.
Euripides

It is all one to me if a man comes from Sing Sing or Harvard. We hire a man, not his history.
Henry Ford, Sr.

We look for creativity, compatibility, and a sense of urgency.
Ernest Gallo

When you hire people who are smarter than you are, you prove you are smarter than they are.
Robert H. Grant

There is something that is much more scarce, something finer far, something rarer than ability. It is the ability to recognize ability.
Elbert Hubbard

A prudent man does not make the goat his gardener.
Hungarian Proverb

The first requisite in running a major corporation is the ability to pick good people.
Lee Iacocca

It is easier to appear worthy of positions that we have not got, than of those that we have.

François, Duc de La Rochefoucauld

Unless we put the right man in the right place—unless we make it possible for our workers and executives alike to enjoy a sense of satisfaction in their jobs, our efforts will have been in vain.

Edward R. Stettinius

My gift is picking a terrific talent and providing the atmosphere for them to do their best work.

Geraldine Stutz

The only really smart thing about me is that I know enough to hire men who are smarter than I am.

Charles Walgreen

It takes a wise man to recognize a wise man.

Xenophon

∽ **Research** ∾

A good internal research department is probably better than all the efficiency engineers ever heard of.

Stuart Chase

The best insurance policy for the future of an industry is research, which will help it to foresee future lines of development, to solve its immediate problems, and to improve and cheapen its products.

Sir Harold Hartley

Nothing is so hard, but search will find it out.

Robert Herrick

Research is going out to look for a change instead of waiting for it to come.

Charles Kettering

Research means that you don't know, but are willing to find out.

Charles Kettering

The common facts of today are the products of yesterday's research.

Duncan MacDonald

Research is to see what everybody else has seen, and to think what nobody else has thought.

Albert Szent-Gyorgyi von Nagyrapolt

∾ Responsibility ∾

Who does no more than his duty is not doing his duty.

Bahya ben Joseph

The great developer is responsibility.

Louis D. Brandeis

Do the duty that lies nearest thee.

Thomas Carlyle

Responsibility is the price of greatness.

Sir Winston Churchill

Shirking easily becomes a habit as difficult to throw off as the use of drugs, and has ruined many men's chances for success.

Henry L. Doherty

Knowledge of your duties is the most essential part of the philosophy of life. If you avoid duty, you avoid action. The world demands results.

George W. Goethels

And what is your duty? Whatever the day calls for.

Johann Wolfgang von Goethe

Responsibilities gravitate to the person who can shoulder them.

Elbert Hubbard

Some people grow under responsibility, others merely swell.

Carl Hubbell

You can't escape the responsibility of tomorrow by evading it today.

Abraham Lincoln

A duty dodged is like a debt unpaid; it is only deferred, and
we must come back and settle
the account at last.

Joseph Fort Newton

Life always gets harder toward
the summit—the cold increases,
responsibility increases.

Friedrich Wilhelm Nietzsche

For great responsibilities there
is a great reward.

Sallust

It is easy to dodge our responsibilities, but we cannot dodge
the consequences of dodging
our responsibilities.

Sir Josiah Stamp

If you can't stand the heat,
stay out of the kitchen.

Harry S. Truman

It is our responsibilities, not
ourselves, that we should take
seriously.

Peter Ustinov

Life is the acceptance of responsibilities or their evasion; it is a
business of meeting obligations
or avoiding them. To every
man the choice is continually
being offered, and by the man-
ner of his choosing you may
fairly measure him.

Ben Ames Williams

There is a single reason why 99
out of 100 average business
men never become leaders.
That is their unwillingness to
pay the price of responsibility.

Owen D. Young

≈ **Results** ≈

Planning is essential for success
but it is results that pay off.

Harry F. Banks

It doesn't matter whether the
cat is black or white, it is a
good cat as long as it catches
mice.

Deng Xiaoping

The greatest results in life are usually attained by simple means and the exercise of ordinary qualities. These may for the most part be summed up in these two—common sense and perseverance.

Owen Feltham

Well done is better than well said.

Benjamin Franklin

When we do our work with a dynamic conquering spirit we get things done.

Arland Gilbert

Half effort does not produce half results. It produces no results. Work, continuous work and hard work, is the only way to accomplish results that last.

Hamilton Holt

Fifty productive men are better than two hundred who art not.

Talmud

The biggest reward for a thing well done is to have done it.

Voltaire

∾ **Risk** ∾

He most prevails who nobly dares.

William Broome

Take a chance! All life is a chance. The man who goes furthest is generally the one who is willing to do and dare. The "sure thing" boat never gets far from shore.

Dale Carnegie

Behold the turtle. He makes progress only when he sticks his neck out.

James Bryant Conant

We must dare, and dare again, and go on daring.

Georges Jacques Danton

You never accumulate if you don't speculate.

David Dodge

All business proceeds on beliefs, on judgments of probabilities, and not on certainties.

Charles William Eliot

Don't be afraid to take a big step if one is indicated; you can't cross a chasm in two small jumps.

Lloyd George

Great profits, great risks.

German Proverb

All men's gains are the fruit of venturing.

Herodotus

Great successes never come without risks.

Flavius Josephus

During the first period of a man's life, the greatest danger is: not to take the risk.

Sören Kierkegaard

Every noble acquisition is attended with its risks; he who fears to encounter the one must not expect to obtain the other.

Pietro Metastasio

First ponder, then dare.

Helmuth von Moltke

Take calculated risks. That is quite different from being rash.

General George S. Patton

Show me a person who isn't taking risks. I'll show you a person who isn't running a business.

Allen E. Paulson

The market and this country were built on risk.

Donald T. Regan

Isn't risk-taking what business is all about?

Frederick W. Smith

Let the man who has to make his fortune in life remember this maxim: Attacking is the only secret. Dare and the world always yields; or if it beats you sometimes, dare it again and it will succumb.

William Makepeace Thackeray

The fact is that you can't get anywhere without taking risks.

Walter Wriston

The whole land must be watered with the streams of knowledge.

Horace Mann

⸎ Salesmanship ⸎

In the word *Business,* the letter "U" comes before the letter "I."

Anonymous

Believe first in what you sell. Believe your prospect will profit by it.

George J. Barnes

Win hearts, and you have all men's hands and purses.

William Henry Burleigh

It's just a step from making a customer willing to hear what you have to say, to making him willing to miss what you have to say.

Frank Farrington

Give the lady what she wants.

Frederick W. Field

Believe the sale really begins *after* the sale—not before.

Joe Girard

Salesmanship consists of transferring a conviction by a seller to a buyer.

Paul G. Hoffman

A real salesman does not attempt to sell his prospect but instead directs his efforts towards putting the prospect in a frame of mind so that he will be moved to action by a given set of facts.

Ray Howard

159

If you were to list the one hundred most successful business organizations in America, I am sure you would find that the great majority of them are successful because they have employed unique or intensive sales methods.

Walton Jones

Stripped of non-essentials, all business activity is a sales battle. And everyone in business must be a salesman.

Robert E. McCowie

A salesman is got to dream, boy. It comes with the territory.

Arthur Miller

Salesmen must act as if they are on the customer's payroll.

Buck Rodger

We are all salesmen every day of our lives. We are selling our ideas, our plans, our enthusiasms to those with whom we come in contact.

Charles M. Schwab

In baseball, the indicator of greatness is the batting average. In the world of sales, it's the closing average.

Clement Stone

Don't sell yourself, sell your company.

Lew Wasserman

∽   **Self-Reliance**   ∽

The gods help them that help themselves.

Aesop

The highest manifestation of life consists in this: That a being governs its own actions.

Saint Thomas Aquinas

No bird soars too high, if he soars with his own wings.

William Blake

Every man is his own architect.

Robert Browning

The highest of all possessions, self-help.

Thomas Carlyle

No fate, nor chance, nor any star commands success and failure—naught but your own hands.

Samuel V. Cole

He who requires much from himself and little from others will be secure.

Confucius

We are the builders of our fortunes.

Ralph Waldo Emerson

Chop your own wood, and it will warm you twice.

Henry Ford, Sr.

Learn to repeat endlessly to yourself, "It all depends on me."

André Gide

One's own hand is the surest and promptest help.

Jean de La Fontaine

The greatest thing in the world is to know how to be self-sufficient.

Montaigne

If ye would go up high, then use your own legs! Do not get yourselves *carried* aloft; do not seat yourselves on other people's backs and heads.

Friedrich Wilhelm Nietzsche

I am myself my own commander.

Plautus

Man is nothing else but what he makes of himself.

Jean Paul Sartre

Let this be your motto—Rely on yourself.

John Godfrey Saxe

The spirit of self-help is the root of all genuine growth in the individual.

Samuel Smiles

For man is man and master of his fate.

Alfred, Lord Tennyson

∽ Selling ∾

We have to watch that we don't try to sell our customers what we think they should have instead of what they really want.

Joseph A. Albertson

Nothing happens until you get a purchase order.

Anonymous

All human relationships are based upon selling of one kind or another, and we all engage in it whenever we undertake to persuade others to our way of thinking.

Claude Briston

Any fool can paint a picture, but it takes a wise man to be able to sell it.

Samuel Butler

A man without a smiling face must not open a shop.

Chinese Proverb

I believe, absolutely, that truth is the strongest and most powerful weapon a man can use, whether he is fighting for a reform or fighting for a sale.

Arthur Dunn

He'll ne'er get a pennysworth that is afraid to ask a price.

Thomas Fuller

He who findeth fault meaneth to buy.

Thomas Fuller

In order to sell, a salesman must firmly believe that the person on the other end of the pitch will actually benefit from the product.

Victor Kiam

In order to sell your product, you don't so much point out its merits as you first work like hell to sell yourself.

Louis Kronenberger

People are usually more convinced by reasons they discovered themselves than by those found by others.

Blaise Pascal

In the factory we make cosmetics. In the store we sell hope.

Charles Revson

Everyone lives by selling something.
>*Robert Louis Stevenson*

The art of assisting discovery.
>*Mark Van Doren*

Don't spend too much time
studying the science of salesmanship. Spend more time
practicing the art of selling.
>*Thomas Watson*

∽ Simplicity ∽

The essence of all good strategy
is simplicity.
>*Eric Ambler*

KISS: Keep It Simple, Stupid.
>*Anonymous*

Out of intense complexities intense simplicities emerge.
>*Sir Winston Churchill*

Everything should be made as
simple as possible, but not sim-
pler.
>*Albert Einstein*

Knowledge is a process of pil-
ing up facts; wisdom lies in
their simplification.
>*Martin H. Fischer*

The obvious is that which is
never seen until someone ex-
presses it simply.
>*Kahlil Gibran*

The higher the truth the sim-
pler it is.
>*Abraham Kook*

Order and simplification are
the first steps toward the mas-
tery of a subject.
>*Thomas Mann*

Any intelligent fool can make
things bigger, more complex. It
takes a touch of genius—and a
lot of courage—to move in the
opposite direction.
>*E.F. Schumacher*

Our life is frittered away by detail. Simplify, simplify.
>*Henry David Thoreau*

There is no greatness where there is not simplicity.

Leo Tolstoy

Less is more.

Ludwig Mies Van der Rohe

When a thought is too weak to be expressed simply, simply drop it.

Luc de Clapiers, Maquis de Vauvenargues

～ Sincerity ～

Never was a sincere word utterly lost.

Ralph Waldo Emerson

No man can produce great things who is not thoroughly sincere in dealing with himself.

James Russell Lowell

Sincerity is impossible unless it pervades the whole being; and the pretense of it saps the very foundation of character.

James Russell Lowell

Never has there been one possessed of complete sincerity who did not move others.

Mencius

What a man says should be what he thinks.

Montaigne

～ Skill ～

Skill to do comes of doing.

Ralph Waldo Emerson

Each man cannot be skilled in everything; each has his special excellence.

Euripides

'Tis skill, not strength, that governs a ship.

> *Thomas Fuller*

The winds and waves are always on the side of the best navigators.

> *Edward Gibbon*

Force has no place where there is need of skill.

> *Herodotus*

A man who qualifies himself well for his calling, never fails of employment.

> *Thomas Jefferson*

Skills vary with the man. We must tread a straight path and strive by that which is born in us.

> *Pindar*

Let each man pass his days in that wherein his skill is greatest.

> *Sextus Propertius*

Every man loves what he is good at.

> *Thomas Shadwell*

The man who has a trade may go anywhere.

> *Spanish Proverb*

∾ Speaking ∽

The mind cannot retain what the seat cannot endure.

> *Anonymous*

Let us not fail to speak clearly, frankly, and firmly.

> *Vincent Auriol*

I take the view that if you cannot say what you have to say in twenty minutes, you should go away and write a book about it.

> *Lord Brabazon*

Grasp the subject, the words will follow

> *Cato*

Blessed is the man who, having nothing to say, abstains from giving in words evidence of the fact.

> *George Eliot*

The eloquent man is he who is no beautiful speaker, but who is inwardly and desperately drunk with a certain belief.

> *Ralph Waldo Emerson*

Better say nothing than nothing
to the purpose.

English Proverb

First learn the meaning of what
you say, and then speak.

Epictetus

The whale only gets harpooned
when he spouts.

Henry Lea Hillman

Why don't th' feller who says,
"I'm not a speechmaker," let
it go at that instead o' givin' a
demonstration?

Frank M. Hubbard

There is an end to speech and
limit to the listener's endurance.

M. Ibn Ezra

Speeches measured by the hour
die with the hour.

Thomas Jefferson

What too many orators want in
depth they give you in length.

Montesquieu

It is but a poor eloquence
which only shows that the ora-
tor can talk.

Sir Joshua Reynolds

Do more than talk, say something.

John H. Rhoades

What is the short meaning of
the long speech?

Johann Friedrich von Schiller

Don't talk unless you can improve the silence.

Vermont Proverb

One always speaks badly when
one has nothing to say.

Voltaire

The secret of being tiresome is
to tell everything.

Voltaire

Never rise to speak till you
have something to say; and
when you have said it, cease.

John Witherspoon

∾ Speech ∾

Speak less cleverly but more clearly.

Aristophanes

It is not sufficient to know what one ought to say, but one must also know how to say it.

Aristotle

The less said the better.

Jane Austen

A voice is a second face.

Gerard Bauer

Drawing on my fine command of language, I said nothing.

Robert Benchley

Let your speech be always with grace, seasoned with salt.

Bible

That which is repeated too often becomes insipid and tedious.

Nicholas Boileau-Despréaux

If a thing goes without saying, let it.

Jacob L. Braude

A fool says what he knows, a sage knows what he says.

Simha Bunam

Too much talk will include errors.

Burmese Proverb

Outside noisy, inside empty.

Chinese Proverb

Short words are best and the old words, when short, are best of all.

Sir Winston Churchill

I have noticed that nothing I never said ever did me any harm.

Calvin Coolidge

Let thy speech be better than silence, or be silent.

Dionysius

Speech is power: speech is to persuade, to convert, to compel.

Ralph Waldo Emerson

Before you say what you think, be sure you have.

Malcolm Forbes

Word-carpentry is like any other kind of carpentry: you must join your sentences smoothly.

Anatole France

When you speak to a man, look on his eyes.

Benjamin Franklin

There is always time to add a word, never to withdraw one.

Baltasar Gracián

Be not confused in words, nor rambling in thought.

Chang Heng

To speak out plainly is the better course.

Homer

A man is hid under his tongue.

Ali Ibn Abi Talib

The worst of men is he whose tongue is mightier than his mind.

M. Ibn Ezra

The most valuable of all talents is that of never using two words when one will do.

Thomas Jefferson

In all speech, words and sense are as the body and soul.

Ben Johnson

No glass renders a man's form or likeness so true as his speech.

Ben Johnson

Before using a fine word, make a place for it.

Joseph Joubert

True eloquence consists in saying all that should be said, and that only.

François, Duc de La Rochefoucauld

Trumpet in a herd of elephants; crow in the company of cocks; bleat in a flock of goats.

Malaysian Proverb

Stick to the point, and whenever you can, cut.

W. Somerset Maugham

When we make ourselves understood, we always speak well, and all your fine diction serves no purpose.

Molière

Oratory is just like prostitution: you must have little tricks.

Vittorio Orlando

Pleasant words are the food of love.

Ovid

Continuous eloquence is tedious.

Blaise Pascal

Man's speech is like his life.

Plato

A sage thing is timely silence, and better than any speech.

Plutarch

Things are well-spoken, if they be well-taken.

Henry Porter

As a man speaks, so is he.

Publilius Syrus

Do not say a little in many words but a great deal in a few.

Pythagoras

The picture of the mind.

John Ray

Brevity of language gives width to thought.

Jean Paul Richter

Speak to the point or be still.

Sigfusson Saemund

Brevity is the soul of wit.

William Shakespeare

Mend your speech a little, lest you may mar your fortunes.

William Shakespeare

It is with words as with sunbeams—the more they are condensed, the deeper they burn.

Robert Southey

Remember, every time you open your mouth to talk, your mind walks out and parades up and down the words.

Edwin H. Stuart

It is man determines what is said, not the words.

Henry David Thoreau

The difference between the right word and the almost right word is the difference between the lightning and the lightning bug.

Mark Twain

Everything that can be said can be said clearly.

Ludwig Wittgenstein

Address another man in the language he understands; do not use literary speech with the uneducated, nor vulgarity with the learned.

Zohar

From a man's mouth you can tell who he is.

Zohar

∽ Statistics ∽

A group of numbers looking for an argument.

Anonymous

Statistics are no substitute for judgment.

Henry Clay

I could prove God statistically.

George Gallup

Then there is the man who drowned crossing a stream with an average depth of six inches.

W. I. E. Gates

He uses statistics as a drunken man uses lampposts—for support rather than for illumination.

Andrew Land

Statistics are like a bikini. What they reveal is suggestive, but what they conceal is vital.

Aaron Levenstein

Statistics are to a speech what lumps are to mashed potatoes; the fewer the better.

J. Lewis Powell

There are two kinds of statistics, the kind you look up and the kind you make up.

Rex Stout

I always find that statistics are hard to swallow and impossible to digest. The only one I can even remember is that if all the people who go to sleep in church were laid end to end they would be a lot more comfortable.

Mrs. Robert A. Taft

❧ **Success** ❧

Work like hell and give the customers what they want.

Joseph A. Albertson

Elbow grease is still the best lubricant for success.

Anonymous

Little successes pave the way to bigger successes.

Mary Kay Ash

Courage to start and willingness to keep everlastingly at it are the requisites for success.

Alonzo Newton Benn

Never mind what others do; do better than yourself, beat your own record from day to day, and you are a success.

William J.H. Boetcker

To be successful, you have to get a charge out of risk-taking. The competitive spirit, pushing to the brink, that's what it's all about.

John F. Bookout, Jr.

Successful minds work like a gimlet—to a single point.

Christian Bovee

Rule No. 1: Never lose money. Rule No. 2: Never forget Rule No. 1.

Warren Edward Buffett

Experience shows that success is due less to ability than to zeal. The winner is he who gives himself to his work, body and soul.

Charles Buxton

Success doesn't come to the sleeper.

Charles Cahier

It takes twenty years to make an overnight success.

Eddie Cantor

I believe the true road to preeminent success in any line is to make yourself master in that line.

Andrew Carnegie

Success depends on previous preparation, and without such preparation there is sure to be failure.

Confucius

When prosperity comes, do not use all of it.

Confucius

There is a master key to success with which no man can fail. Its name is simplicity. Simplicity, I mean, in the sense of reducing to the simplest possible terms every problem that besets us.

Henri Deterding

Presence of mind and courage in distress are more than armies to procure success.

John Dryden

Nothing succeeds like success.

Alexandre Dumas, the Younger

I see more and more that honesty in word, thought, and work means success. It spells a life worth living and in business, clean success.

George Eberhard

The one common characteristic that all successful people share is that they have their goals and their life outlined in writing.

J. Douglas Edward

If A equals success, then the formula is A equals X plus Y plus Z. X is work. Y is play. Z is keep your mouth shut.

Albert Einstein

It is never too late to be what you might have been.

George Eliot

A determination to succeed is the only way to succeed.

William Feather

Nothing is more humiliating than to see idiots succeed in enterprises we have failed in.

Gustave Flaubert

The great majority of conspicuously successful men are early risers. To get up in the world, get up early in the morning.

B. C. Forbes

It's easier to grab success than to hold on to it.

Malcolm Forbes

Success is a matter of adjusting one's efforts to obstacles and one's abilities to a service needed by others.

Henry Ford, Sr.

The man who will use his skill and constructive imagination to see how much he can give for a dollar, instead of how little he can give for a dollar, is bound to succeed.

Henry Ford

If you want to succeed in the world you must make your own opportunities as you go on. The man who waits for some seventh wave to toss him on dry land will find that the seventh wave is a long time coming.

John B. Gough

He started to sing as he tackled the thing that couldn't be done, and he did it.

Edgar A. Guest

Character is the real foundation of all worthwhile success.

John Hammond

Every man should make up his mind that if he expects to succeed, he must give an honest return for the other man's dollar.

Edward H. Harriman

'Tis a lesson you should heed, try, try again. If at first you don't succeed, try, try again.

William E. Hickson

Success comes to those who become success conscious. Failure comes to those who indifferently allow themselves to become failure conscious.

Napoleon Hill

Something that I have strictly adhered to is to have integrity, never under any circumstances to deceive anybody, to have your word good.

Conrad Hilton

People succeed because they believe, not only that they can and will succeed, but also that success is worth the price they must pay for it.

Tom Hopkins

If you succeed in life, you must do it in spite of the efforts of others to pull you down. There is nothing in the idea that people are willing to help those who help themselves.

Edgar Watson Howe

Stability is more essential to success than brilliancy.

Richard Lloyd Jones

Nature gave men two ends— one to sit on and one to think with. Ever since then man's success or failure has been dependent on the one he used most.

George R. Kirkpatrick

Success is the greatest thing in the world—I'll tell you why. Without it, a man is a failure.

Clare Kummer

To succeed in the world, we do everything we can to appear successful.

François, Duc de La Rochefoucauld

Let no feeling of discouragement prey upon you, and in the end you are sure to succeed.

Abraham Lincoln

The successful people are the ones who can think up things for the rest of the world to keep busy at.

Don Marquis

The ability to form friendships, to make people believe in you and trust in you, is one of the few absolutely fundamental qualities of success.

John J. McGuirk

The young man who would succeed must identify his interest with those of his employer and exercise the same diligence in matters entrusted to him as he would in his own affairs.

Louis Mercier

Nothing is impossible to the man who can will, and then do.

Honoré Gabriel Riquetti, Comte de Mirabeau

Successful businessmen share the ability to hire people smarter than they are.

Dillard Munford

Half the things that people do not succeed in are through fear of making the attempt.

James Northgate

The very first step towards success in any occupation is to become interested in it.

Sir William Osler

The art of dealing with people is the foremost secret of successful men.

Paul C. Packer

Will opens the door to success.

Louis Pasteur

If at first you don't succeed, you have plenty of company.

Eldon Pedersen

Vigilance in watching opportunity; tack and daring in seizing upon opportunity; force and persistence in crowding opportunity to its utmost possible achievement—these are the martial virtues which must command success.

Austin Phelps

I can give you a six-word formula for success: "Think things through—then follow through."

Edward Rickenbacker

If you want to succeed you should strike out on new paths rather than travel the worn paths of accepted success.

John D. Rockefeller, Sr.

The only place where success comes before work is in a dictionary.

Vidal Sassoon

The difference between failure and success is doing a thing nearly right and doing it exactly right.

Edward C. Simmons

The successful person is the one who went ahead and did the thing I always intended to do.

Ruth Smeltzer

I cannot give you the formula for success, but I can give you the formula for failure—which is: Try to please everybody.

Herbert Bayard Swope

Only he is successful in his business who makes that pursuit which affords him the highest pleasure sustain him.

Henry David Thoreau

Success usually comes to those who are too busy to be looking for it.

Henry David Thoreau

Let us be thankful for the fools. But for them the rest of us could not succeed.

Mark Twain

We never know, believe me, when we have succeeded best.

Miguel de Unamuno

There is always something about your success that displeases even your best friends.

Oscar Wilde

Success begins with a fellow's will.

Walter Wintle

Success is not the reverse of failure; it is the scorn of failure. Always dare to fail; never fail to dare.

Stephen S. Wise

On the door to success it says: push and pull.

Yiddish Proverb

ᶜᵃ Success (Definition) ᶜᵃ

The best revenge.

Anonymous

The ability to convert ideas to things.

Henry Ward Beecher

Constancy to purpose.

Benjamin Disraeli

The child of audacity.

Benjamin Disraeli

Finding a better method.

Ralph Waldo Emerson

The sum of detail.

Harvey Firestone

A result, not a goal.

Gustave Flaubert

Ideas exclusively focused on one central interest.

Sigmund Freud

Good management in action.

William E. Holler

The result of mental attitude.

Oliver Wendell Holmes, Sr.

Doing, not wishing.

Tom Hopkins

Your birthright.

Grenville Kleiser

Concentrating all efforts at all times upon one point.

Ferdinand Lassalle

That old ABC—Ability, Breaks, and Courage.

Charles Luckman

Failure kicked to pieces by hard work.

Jimmy Lyons

Knowing how to get along with people.

Theodore Roosevelt

Sinning on purpose.

Robert Schillaci

The reward of toil.

Sophocles

A journey, not a destination.

Ben Sweetland

Understanding of the world about you and then making products to fit the needs of the times.

Pieter C. Vink

A matter of luck. Ask any failure.

Earl Wilson

The reward of anyone who looks for trouble.

Walter Winchell

Quotations when engraved upon the memory give you good thoughts.

Sir Winston Churchill

∽ Tact ∽

Closing your mouth before someone feels the urge to.

Anonymous

Tact is like a girdle. It enables you to organize the awkward truth more attractively.

Anonymous

Tact consists in knowing how far to go too far.

Jean Cocteau

Difficulties melt away under tact.

Benjamin Disraeli

Whenever you find anyone who is outstandingly successful and popular, you will find a person who is outstandingly tactful.

Donald A. Laird

Tact is the ability to describe others as they see themselves.

Abraham Lincoln

The knack of letting the other fellow have your way.

Abraham Lincoln

Tact is the art of making a point without making an enemy.

Howard W. Newton

The unsaid part of what you think.

Henry Van Dyke

∾ Talent ∾

Talent is only a starting point in business. You've got to keep working that talent.

Irving Berlin

If every man stuck to his talent, the cows would be well tended.

J.P. Claris de Florian

The world is always ready to receive talent with open arms.

Oliver Wendell Holmes, Sr.

Everyone has talent. What is rare is the courage to follow the talent to where it leads.

Erica Jong

It is not enough to have great qualities, we should also have the management of them.

François, Duc de La Rochefoucauld

Nature has concealed at the bottom of our minds talents and abilities of which we are not aware.

François, Duc de La Rochefoucauld

Whatever you are from nature, keep to it; never desert your own line of talent. Be what nature intended you for, and you will succeed.

Sydney Smith

There is probably no man living, though ever so great a fool, that cannot do *something* or other well.

Samuel Warren

What can any of us do with his talent but try to develop his vision, so that through frequent failures we may learn better what we have missed in the past.

William Carlos Williams

If a man has a talent and learns somehow to use the whole of it, he has gloriously succeeded, and won a satisfaction and a triumph few men will ever know.

Thomas Wolfe

The real tragedy of life is not in being limited to one talent, but in the failure to use the one talent.

Edgar W. Work

∾ **Tax** ∾

Taxing is an easy business, but is it altogether wise to have no other bounds to your impositions than the patience of those who are to bear them?

Edmund Burke

The imposition of taxes has its limits. There is a maximum which cannot be transcended.

Henry Clay

The art of taxation consists in so plucking the goose as to obtain the largest possible amount of feathers with the smallest possible amount of hissing.

Jean Baptiste Colbert

The point to remember is that what the government gives it must first take away.

John S. Coleman

Collecting more taxes than is absolutely necessary is legalized robbery.

Calvin Coolidge

I do not believe that the government should ask social legislation in the guise of taxation. If we are to adopt socialism, it should be presented to the people of this country as socialism and not under the guise of a law to collect revenue.

Calvin Coolidge

I'm proud to be paying taxes in the United States. The only thing is—I could be just as proud for half the money.

Arthur Godfrey

The power to tax is not the power to destroy while this court sits.

Oliver Wendell Holmes, Jr.

I want to be the President who helped to feed the hungry and to prepare them to be taxpayers instead of tax eaters.

Lyndon B. Johnson

The power to tax involves the power to destroy.

Chief Justice John Marshall

If Patrick Henry thought that taxation without representation was bad, he should see how bad it is with representation.

The Old Farmer's Almanac

There is no art which one government sooner learns of another than that of draining money from the pockets of the people.

Adam Smith

It is the part of a good shepherd to shear his flock, not flay it.

Tiberius

～ **Teamwork** ⌒

All for one, and one for all.

Alexandre Dumas, the Younger

No member of a crew is praised for rugged individuality of his rowing.

Ralph Waldo Emerson

Coming together is a beginning; keeping together is progress; working together is success.

Henry Ford, Sr.

The welfare of every business is dependent upon cooperation and teamwork on the part of its personnel.

Charles Gow

Each of us *is* the company.

William Hewlett

Everyone is part of a team. Achievements are the results of the combined efforts of each individual.

William Hewlett

Light is the task where many
share the toil.

Homer

A major reason capable people
fail to advance is that they
don't work well with their col-
leagues.

Lee Iacocca

Productivity gains come from
improved coordination rather
than from increased physical effort (when) all employees willingly engage in analysis, planning, and decision making.

William Ouchi

The multitude which does not
reduce itself to unity is confusion.

Blaise Pascal

We are all dependent on one
another, every soul of us on
earth.

George Bernard Shaw

We are apt to forget that we
are only one of a team; that in
unity there is strength and that
we are strong only as long as
each unit in our organization
functions with precision.

Samuel J. Tilden

～ **Thinking** ～

The brain is as strong as its
weakest think.

Anonymous

Whether you want to make
money, or write a book, or
build a bridge, or run a street-
car—or do anything else successfully—you'll do well to remember that in all the world
there is no word more important than "think."

Edwin Baird

The shrewd guess, the fertile
hypothesis, the courageous leap
to a tentative conclusion—these
are the most valuable coin of
the thinker at work.

Jerome S. Bruner

When everyone thinks alike,
few are doing much thinking.

Nashua Cavalier

Creative thinking is today's most prized, profit-producing possession for an individual, corporation, or country.

Robert P. Crawford

Thinking is hard work.

Thomas Alva Edison

The best thinking has been done in solitude. The worst has been done in turmoil.

Thomas Alva Edison

Thinking is the hardest work there is, which is the probable reason why so few engage in it.

Henry Ford, Sr.

We must dare to think "unthinkable" thoughts. We must learn to explore all the options and possibilities that confront us in a complex and rapidly changing world.

James W. Fulbright

Those that think must govern those that toil.

Oliver Goldsmith

He that thinks amiss concludes worse.

George Herbert

He thinks not well that thinks not again.

George Herbert

Think and grow rich.

Napoleon Hill

The success or failure of every business enterprise is traceable to one source, and one source only, namely, somebody's mind, for no one has yet invented a machine that can think.

Henning W. Prentis, Jr.

To think is not enough; you must think of something.

Jules Renard

To think is to converse with oneself.

Miguel de Unamuno

It is not much good thinking of a thing unless you think it out.

H. G. Wells

∾ **Thought** ∾

Millions say the apple fell but
Newton was the one to ask why.

Bernard M. Baruch

Men are not influenced by
things, but by their thoughts
about things.

Epictetus

Thought, not money, is the
real business capital.

Harvey Firestone

The mind is an iceberg—it
floats with only one-seventh of
its bulk above water.

Sigmund Freud

Great thoughts reduced to practice become great acts.

William Hazlitt

The mind grows by what it
feeds on.

Josiah Gilbert Holland

Too often we enjoy the comfort
of opinion without the discomfort of thought.

John F. Kennedy

How many ideas hover dis-
persed in my head of which
many a pair if they should
come together, could bring
about the greatest of discoveries!

Georg Christoph Lichtenberg

The thoughts that come often
unsought are commonly the
most valuable of any we have,
and therefore should be secured, because they seldom return again.

John Locke

What I have done is due to pa-
tient thought.

Sir Isaac Newton

Change your thoughts and you
change your world.

Norman Vincent Peale

Human thought, like God,
makes the world in its own
image.

Adam Clayton Powell, Jr.

Thought breeds thought.

Henry David Thoreau

When a thought is too weak to
be expressed simply, it should
be rejected.

*Luc de Clapiers, Marquis de
Vauvenargues*

Iron rusts from disuse, stagnant water loses its purity, and
in cold weather becomes fro-
zen; even so does inaction sap
the vigors of the mind.

Leonardo da Vinci

Human thought is the process by which human ends are ultimately answered.

Daniel Webster

We need to cultivate fertility in thought as we have cultivated efficiency in administration.

Norbert Wiener

∾ Time ∾

We cannot waste time. We can only waste ourselves.

George Adams

To ''kill time'' is—by definition—to murder it.

Anonymous

To choose time is to save time.

Francis Bacon

A man must be master of his hours and days, not their servant.

William Frederick Book

You will never ''find'' time for anything. If you want time, you must make it.

Charles Buxton

Regret for time wasted can become a power for good in the time that remains.

Arthur Brisbane

Know the true value of time; snatch, seize, and enjoy every moment of it. No idleness, no laziness or procrastination.

Philip Dormer Stanhope, Earl of Chesterfield

The less one has to do, the less time one finds to do it in.

Philip Dormer Stanhope, Earl of Chesterfield

An inch of gold will not buy an inch of time.

Chinese Proverb

Everyone has his day and some days last longer than others.

Sir Winston Churchill

Much may be done in those little shreds and patches of time which every day produces and which most men throw away.

Charles Caleb Colton

The present time has one advantage over every other; it is our own.

Charles Caleb Colton

It is the wisest who grieve most at the loss of time.

Dante Alighieri

Time is really the only capital that any human being has, and the one thing that he can't afford to lose.

Thomas Alva Edison

From time waste there can be no salvage. It is the easiest of all to waste and the hardest to correct because it does not litter the floor.

Henry Ford, Sr.

He who rises late may trot all day, and not overtake his business at night.

Benjamin Franklin

A little too late is much too late.

German Proverb

There are no office hours for leaders.

Cardinal James Gibbons

Nothing is worth more than this day.

Johann Wolfgang von Goethe

Each day a day goes by.

Carlo Goldoni

At the beginning of every day we're all given 86,400 seconds. As each one ticks by, we've lost it forever in every way unless we find a way to invest that moment in the future.

Tom Hopkins

Our greatest danger in life is in permitting the urgent things to crowd out the important.

Charles E. Hummel

No person will have occasion to complain of the want of time, who never loses any.

Thomas Jefferson

Time is a fixed income and, as with any income, the real problem facing most of us is how to live successfully within our daily allotment.

Margaret B. Johnstone

Every man's greatest capital asset is his unexpired years of productive life.

Paul W. Litchfield

Nothing inspires confidence in a business sooner than punctuality, nor is there any habit which sooner saps his reputation than that of being always behind time.

William Mathews

Don't be fooled by the calendar. There are only as many days in the year as you make use of. One man gets only a week's value out of a year while another man gets a full year's value out of a week.

Charles Richards

It takes time to succeed because success is merely the natural reward for taking time to do anything well.

Joseph Ross

Make use of time, let not advantage slip.

William Shakespeare

Those who have most to do, and are willing to work, will find the most time.

Samuel Smiles

You are not born for fame if you don't know the value of time.

Luc de Clapiers, Marquis de Vauvenargues

Reason, too late perhaps, may convince you of the folly of misspending time.

George Washington

My rule always was to do the business of the day in the day.

Arthur Wellesley, Duke of Wellington

∾ Time (Definition) ∾

Time is the measure of business, as money is of wares.

Francis Bacon

The stuff life's made of.

David Belasco

Time, O my friend, is money!

Edward George Bulwer-Lytton

A ripener. No man is born wise.

Miguel de Cervantes

What we want most, but what we use worst.

William Penn

The wisest counselor of all.

Pericles

The most valuable thing a man can spend.

Theophrastus

∾ Timing ∾

This time like all times is a
very good one if we but know
what to do with it.

Ralph Waldo Emerson

When the iron is hot, strike.

John Heywood

Don't cross the bridge till you
come to it.

Henry Wadsworth Longfellow

You should hammer your iron
when it is glowing hot.

Publilius Syrus

There is a slowness in affairs
which ripens them, and a slowness which rots them.

Joseph Roux

∾ Trade ∾

Free trade, one of the greatest
blessings which a government
can confer on a people, is in almost every country unpopular.

Thomas Babington

We live in a world of trade.

John B. Connaly, Jr.

Trade should be free, even in
Hell.

Danish Proverb

Trade which, like blood, should
circularly flow.

John Dryden

I am for free commerce with all
nations.

Thomas Jefferson

∾ **Trends** ∾

All things grow old through
time.

Aristotle

The most important thing is to
seize a trend.

Michael C. Bergerac

Every trend plants the seeds of
the next one.

Tom Hopkins

For every trend there is often
an equally compelling coun-
tertrend.

John Naisbitt

Trends are generated from the
bottom up, fads from the top
down.

John Naisbitt

Trends, like horses, are easier
to ride in the direction they are
already going.

John Naisbitt

A great man quotes bravely, and will not draw
on his invention when his memory serves him
with a word so good.

Ralph Waldo Emerson

◦ Unions ◦

In the last six centuries the la-
boring population has risen
from a condition of serfdom to
a state of political freedom.
Where they did not pursue
their interest, they lost their interest. Their weapons were the
strike and the trade union.

Thomas S. Adams

Self-defense drove him to union
with his fellows.

Edward Bellamy

Only a fool would try to de-
prive working men and women
of the right to join the union of
their choice.

Dwight D. Eisenhower

Show me the country in which
there are no strikes and I'll
show you that country in which
there is no liberty.

Samuel Gompers

The power developed by combination (union) may be abused,
like any other power; but labor
is helpless and a prey without it.

Horace Greeley

No private business monopoly,
producer organization, or cartel
wields the market power or
commands the discipline over
its members which many
unions have achieved.

Gottfried Haberler

Union leaders who convince the workman that his employer is his natural enemy serve only the Marxian doctrine.

Herbert B. Kohler

We may lay it down as a general and lasting law that working-men's associations should be so organized and governed as to furnish the best and most suitable means for attaining what is aimed at.

Pope Leo XIII

Unionism seldom, if ever, uses such power as it has to insure better work; almost always it devotes a large part of that power to safeguarding bad work.

H. L. Mencken

It is one of the characteristics of a free and democratic modern nation that it have free and independent labor unions.

Franklin D. Roosevelt

Union is essential to give laborers opportunity to deal on an equality with their employer.

U.S. Supreme Court

❧ Understanding ❧

One who understands much displays a greater simplicity of character than one who understands little.

Alexander Chase

Understanding is the beginning of approving.

André Gide

A moment's insight is sometimes worth a life's experience.

Oliver Wendell Holmes, Sr.

Mediocre minds usually dismiss anything which reaches beyond their own understanding.

François, Duc de La Rochefoucauld

Until we know what motivates the hearts and minds of men we can understand nothing outside ourselves.

Marya Mannes

I do not understand; I pause; I examine.

Montaigne

One learns peoples through the heart, not the eyes or the intellect.

Mark Twain

Nothing can be loved or hated unless it is first known.

Leonardo da Vinci

Sensible men show their sense by saying much
in few words.

Charles Simmons

∽ **Value** ∾

The price is what you pay, the
value is what you receive.

Anonymous

What you get free costs too
much.

Jean Anouilh

You get what you pay for.

Gabriel Biel

When a customer buys a low-
grade article, he feels pleased
when he pays for it and is
pleased every time he uses it.
But when he buys a well-made
article, he feels extravagant
when he pays for it and well
pleased every time he uses it.

Herbert N. Casson

What costs little is valued less.

Miguel de Cervantes

As good as gold.

Charles Dickens

When the well's dry, we know
the worth of water.

Benjamin Franklin

The greatest gift is the power
to estimate correctly the value
of things.

*François, Duc de La
Rochefoucauld*

193

Things are only worth what
one makes them worth.

Molière

Everything is worth what its
purchaser will pay for it.

Publilius Syrus

∽ **Vision** ∾

The farther backward you can
look, the farther forward you
are likely to see.

Sir Winston Churchill

A rock pile ceases to be a rock
pile the moment a single man
contemplates it, bearing within
him the image of a cathedral.

Antoine de Saint-Exupéry

What you look for is what
you'll see.

Malcolm Forbes

The vision of things to be done
may come a long time before
the way of doing them becomes
clear, but woe to him who dis-
trusts the vision.

Jenkin Lloyd Jones

A man to carry on a successful
business must have imagination. He must see things in a vision, a dream of the whole
thing.

Charles M. Schwab

You see things, and you say
"why?"; but I dream things
that never were, and I say
"why not?"

George Bernard Shaw

We must stop assuming that a
thing which has never been
done before probably cannot be
done at all.

Donald M. Nelson

Vision is the art of seeing
things invisible.

Jonathan Swift

Sayings which combine sense, shortness, and salt.

James Howell

∽ **Wages** ∽

The big salaries in business always go to those who have what it takes to get things done.

John C. Aspley

A fair day's wage for a fair day's work: it is as just a demand as governed men ever made of governing.

Thomas Carlyle

It is not the employer who pays wages—he only handles the money. It is the product that pays wages.

Henry Ford, Sr.

If you cut wages, you just cut the number of your customers.

Henry Ford, Sr.

All too much of the wage structure has been based on the time workers put in, rather than upon the product put out.

Wheeler McMillen

Wages should be left to the fair and free competition of the market, and should never be controlled by the interference of the legislature.

David Ricardo

One man's wage increase is another man's price increase.

Sir Harold Wilson

∾ Wealth ∾

Truly wealth is a sweet and pleasant thing.

Aristophanes

A large income is the best recipe for happiness I ever heard of.

Jane Austen

If a man look sharply and attentively, he shall see fortune; for though she is blind, she is not invisible.

Francis Bacon

The pursuit of wealth is one of life's most fascinating journeys, especially when you catch up with it.

Baron's Advertisement

Riches are not an end of life, but an instrument of life.

Henry Ward Beecher

It is the interest of the commercial world that wealth should be found everywhere.

Edmund Burke

The masses of the people in any country are prosperous and comfortable just in proportion as there are millionaires.

Andrew Carnegie

All wealth lies in increased production.

Fred C. Crawford

All heiresses are beautiful.

John Dryden

Fortune favors the audacious.

Desiderius Erasmus

The thing most honored among men, and the source of the greatest power.

Euripides

The real limits to your wealth are as much a matter of determination and willpower as of skill.

Kenneth L. Fisher

In short, the way to wealth, if you desire it, depends chiefly on two words, industry and frugality; that is, waste neither time nor money, but make the best use of both.

Benjamin Franklin

I believe that the able industrial leader who creates wealth and employment is more worthy of historical notice than politicians or soldiers.

J. Paul Getty

Enrich yourselves.

François Guizot

It is better to live rich than to die rich.

Samuel Johnson

Wealth depends upon commerce, and commerce depends upon circulation.

John Law

We shall never solve the paradox of want in the midst of plenty by doing away with plenty.

Ogden Mills

Those who condemn wealth are those who have none and see no chance of getting it.

William Penn Patrick

Wealth is the product of man's capacity to think.

Ayn Rand

In a country where there are no rich there will be only the poor—the very poor.

Walter Rathenau

The only question with wealth is what you do with it.

John D. Rockefeller, Jr.

The use of riches is better than their possession.

Fernando de Rojas

It requires a great deal of boldness and a great deal of caution to make a great fortune; and when you have got it, it requires ten times as much wit to keep it.

Meyer Rothschild

Why is one man richer than another? Because he is more industrious, more persevering, and more sagacious.

John Ruskin

Remember, it's as easy to marry a rich woman as a poor woman.

William Makepeace Thackeray

I've been rich and I've been poor; rich is better.

Sophie Tucker

A rich man has not only money, he has credit too.

Yiddish Proverb

～ **Will** ～

Where there's a will there's a way.

English Proverb

Victory is a thing of the will.

Ferdinand Foch

The world is full of willing people; some willing to work, the rest willing to let them.

Robert Frost

He who is firm in will molds the world to himself.

Johann Wolfgang von Goethe

To him that will, ways are not wanting.

George Herbert

Nothing is impossible to a willing heart.

John Heywood

People do not lack strength; they lack will.

Victor Hugo

Where the willingness is great, the difficulties cannot be great.

Nicolò Machiavelli

The unconquerable will.

John Milton

Lack of willpower has caused more failure than lack of intelligence or ability.

Flower A. Newhouse

When there's a will there's a way.

George Bernard Shaw

The will is the man.

John M. Wilson

～ **Winning** ～

No one conquers who doesn't fight.

Gabriel Biel

Expect victory and you make victory. Nowhere is this truer than in business life where bravery and faith bring both material and spiritual rewards.

Preston Bradley

Act as if it were impossible to fail.

Dorothea Brande

Every winner has scars; the men who succeed are the efficient few. They are the few who have the ambition and willpower to develop themselves.

Herbert N. Casson

To win without risk is to triumph without glory.

Pierre Corneille

The last shot may give us the victory.

Admiral Duchayla

Victory is Spirit.

Anatole France

Hit hard, hit fast, and hit often.

William F. Halsey, Jr.

Hard working "todays" make high-winning "tomorrows."

William E. Holler

A matter of staying power.

Elbert Hubbard

Never give up and never give in.

Hubert H. Humphrey

Slow and steady wins the race.

Robert Lloyd

You can't win any game unless you are ready to win.

Connie Mack

If you would win the world, melt it, do not hammer it.

Alexander Maclaren

Refuse to join the cautious crowd that plays not to lose; play to win.

David J. Mahoney

Everything I do, I do to win.

Robert Maxwell

When you win, nothing hurts.

Joe Namath

The lesson that most of us on this voyage never learn, but can never quite forget, is that to win is sometimes to lose.

Richard M. Nixon

Short-range defeats are often long-range victories.

Alexander H. Pekelis

Push, push, push, harder, harder, harder.

H. Ross Perot

One must work, nothing but work.

Auguste Rodin

The conditions of conquest are always easy. We have but to toil awhile, endure awhile, believe always, and never turn back.

Seneca

You must develop a feeling that there's no way you're going to lose.

Roger Staubach

Winning means being unafraid to lose.

Fran Tarkenton

I do not think winning is the most important thing. I think winning is the only thing.

Bill Veek

The most difficult part of getting to the top of the ladder is getting through the crowd at the bottom.

Arch Ward

∾ **Wisdom** ↩

A prudent question is one-half of wisdom.

Francis Bacon

The price of wisdom is eternal thought.

Frank Birch

It may be a mistake to mix different wines, but old and new wisdom mix admirably.

Bertolt Brecht

Wisdom lies in masterful administration of the unforeseen.

Robert Bridges

Be wiser than other people if you can; but do not tell them so.

Philip Dormer Stanhope, Earl of Chesterfield

They call him the wisest man to whose mind that which is required at once occurs.

Marcus Tullius Cicero

The sum of wisdom is, that the time is never lost that is devoted to work.

Ralph Waldo Emerson

To see the miraculous in the common.

Ralph Waldo Emerson

The wise man must be wise before, not after, the event.

Epicharmos

He is wise that follows the wise.

Edward FitzGerald

Abundance of knowledge does not teach men to be wise.

Heraclitus

To read the present right, and profit by the occasion.

Homer

Wisdom consists not so much in knowing what to do in the ultimate as in knowing what to do next.

Herbert Hoover

True wisdom is to know what is best worth knowing, and to do what is best worth doing.

Edward Porter Humphrey

The beginning of wisdom is to desire it.

Solomon ben Judah Ibn Gabirol

The wisdom of the wise is an uncommon degree of common sense.

Dean William Ralph Inge

The art of being wise is the art of knowing what to overlook.

William James

Wisdom is the conqueror of fortune.

Juvenal

Who is wise? He who learns from everybody.

Mishna

I have always observed that to succeed in the world one should appear like a fool but be wise.

Montesquieu

From the errors of others a wise man corrects his own

Publilius Syrus

Nine-tenths of wisdom is being wise in time.

Theodore Roosevelt

Some folks are wise, and some are otherwise.

Tobias Smollett

To know how to use knowledge is wisdom.

Charles H. Spurgeon

Who is wise? He who foresees results.

Talmud

True wisdom consists not only in seeing what is before your eyes, but in foreseeing what is to come.

Terence

❧ **Work** ❧

A work of real merit finds favor at last.

Amos Bronson Alcott

If you think the world owes you a living, hustle out and collect it.

Anonymous

The man who rolls up his shirt sleeves is rarely in danger of losing his shirt.

Anonymous

There aren't any rules for success that work unless you do.

Anita Belmont

Be strong, and work.

Bible

Go to the ant, you sluggard, consider her ways, and be wise.

Bible

I fight Poverty—I work.

Bumper Sticker

Every man's work is always a portrait of himself.

Samuel Butler

All work is a seed sown; it grows and spreads, and sows itself anew.

Thomas Carlyle

Never stand begging for that which you have the power to earn.

Miguel de Cervantes

He who considers his work beneath him will be above doing it well.

Alexander Chase

Never was a good work done
without great effort.

Chinese Proverb

Honor lies in honest toil.

Grover Cleveland

There's only one way to work—
like hell.

Bette Davis

Do all the work you can: that
is the whole philosophy of the
good way of life.

Eugène Delacroix

Possibly we might even improve the world a little, if we
got up early in the morning,
and took off our coats to the
work.

Charles Dickens

As a cure for worrying, work is
better than whiskey.

Thomas Alva Edison

I am wondering what would
have happened to me if some
fluent talker had converted me
to the theory of the eight-hour
day and convinced me that it
was not fair to my fellow workers to put forth my best efforts
in my work.

Thomas Alva Edison

I never did anything worth
doing by accident; nor did any
of my inventions come by accident; they came by work.

Thomas Alva Edison

All work and no play makes
Jack a dull boy—and Jill a
wealthy widow.

Evan Esar

There will never be a system invented which will do away with
the necessity for work.

Henry Ford, Sr.

What is needed is an orderly
transfer from welfare rolls to
payrolls.

Milton Friedman

Life grants nothing to us mor-
tals without hard work.

Horace

If you work for a man, in
heaven's name work for him!

Elbert Hubbard

Your job is only as big as you
are.

George C. Hubbs

Good work is the great charac-
ter-builder, the sweetener of
life, the maker of destiny.

Grenville Kleiser

Our work is our path.

Lao-tzu

There is always work, and tools to work withal, for those who will.

James Russell Lowell

The more a man gives of himself to his work, the more he will get out of it, both in wage and satisfaction.

Joseph T. Mackey

The one way to the top is by persistent, intelligent, hard work.

Armand T. Mercier

Whatever you do, if you do it hard enough you'll enjoy it. The important thing is to work and work hard.

David Rockefeller

When I hear a young man spoken of as giving promise of great genius, the first question I ask about him always is, does he work?

John Ruskin

The best investment a young man starting out in business could possibly make is to give all his time, all his energies to work, just plain, hard work.

Charles M. Schwab

Hire yourself out to work which is beneath you rather than become dependent on others.

Talmud

The great thing with work is to be on top of it, not constantly chasing after it.

Dorothy Thompson

Work is the true source of human welfare.

Leo Tolstoy

He who does not work shall not eat.

Article 12, USSR Constitution of 1936

❧ Select Bibliography ☙

Andrews, Robert. *The Concise Columbia Dictionary of Quotations*. New York: Columbia University Press, 1989.

Ash, Mary Kay. *People Management*. New York: Warner, 1984.

Auden, W. H., and Louis Kronenberger. *The Viking Book of Aphorisms*. New York: Penguin Books, 1984.

Baron, Joseph L. *A Treasury of Jewish Quotations*. South Brunswick: Thomas Yoseloff, 1965.

Bartlett, John. *Familiar Quotations,* 15th edition, edited by Emily Morison Beck. Boston: Little, Brown, 1980.

Bohle, Bruce. *The Home Book of American Quotations*. New York: Gramercy, 1986.

Brussell, Eugene E. *Dictionary of Quotable Definitions*. New York: Prentice Hall, 1970.

_____. *Webster's New World Dictionary of Quotable Definitions*. New York: Prentice Hall, 1988.

Bursk, Edward C., Donald T. Clark, and Ralph W. Hidy. *The World of Business,* 4 volumes. New York: Simon and Schuster, 1962.

Cohen, J. M., and M. J. Cohen. *The Penguin Dictionary of Quotations*. Harmondsworth: Penguin, 1985.

Fergusson, Rosalind. *The Penguin Dictionary of Proverbs*. Harmondsworth: Penguin, 1983.

Forbes, Malcolm S. *The Forbes Scrapbook of Thoughts on the Business of Life,* 2 volumes. New York: B. C. Forbes & Sons, 1984.

Forbes, Malcolm S. *The Further Sayings of Chairman Malcolm*. New York: Harper & Row, 1986.

Heider, John. *The TAO of Leadership*. New York: Bantam, 1985.

Hopkins, Tom. *The Official Guide to Success*. New York: Warner, 1984.

Iacocca, Lee. *Iacocca*. New York: Bantam, 1984.

Kent, Robert W. *Money Talks*. New York: Pocket Books, 1985.

McNeil, Barbara. *Biography and Genealogy Master Index*. Detroit: Gale, 1985.

Naisbitt, John. *Megatrends.* New York: Warner, 1984.

O'Kill, Brian. *Popular Quotations A–Z.* Essex: Longman House, 1985.

The Oxford Book of Aphorisms. Oxford: Oxford University Press, 1983.

The Oxford Dictionary of Quotations. Oxford: Oxford University Press, 1979.

Peter, Lawrence J. *Peter's Quotations.* New York: Bantam Books, 1980.

Peters, Thomas J., and Robert H. Waterman, Jr. *In Search of Excellence.* New York: Warner, 1982.

Pickens, T. Boone, Jr. *Boone.* Boston: Houghton Mifflin, 1987.

Randseep, Eugene. *Quotes.* Los Angeles: Price, Stern, Sloan, 1984.

Seldes, George. *The Great Quotations.* New York: Lyle Stuart, 1960.

Simpson, James B. *Simpson's Contemporary Quotations.* Boston: Houghton Mifflin, 1988.

Stevenson, Burton. *The Macmillan Book of Proverbs, Maxims, and Famous Phrases.* New York: Macmillan, 1987.

Sweeting, George. *Great Quotes and Illustrations.* Waco: Word Books, 1985.

Tripp, Rhoda Thomas. *The International Thesaurus of Quotations.* New York: Thomas Y. Crowell, 1970.

White, Rolf B. *The Last Word on Making Money.* Seacaucus: Lyle Stuart, 1988.

Author/Subject Index

This index contains the names and, where possible, dates of all the persons quoted in this book. Other sources, such as proverbs from various countries, are also listed. Under each listed heading are the topics quoted from that source, and the page numbers where the specific quotes can be found. Anonymous quotes are not listed in this index, but can be located alphabetically within each subject category.

❦ Key Word Index ❧

The key words associated with each quote are listed here. Every effort has been made to include words that will help to locate a favorite or half-forgotten saying. In addition to finding the key words, the reader will discover this to be an in-depth subject index. Broad subject headings can be found in the Table of Contents.

240